MASTERCHEF
1994

MASTERCHEF 1994

FOREWORD BY LOYD GROSSMAN

GENERAL EDITOR: JANET ILLSLEY

VERMILION
LONDON

First published 1994

13 5 7 9 10 8 6 4 2

Compilation copyright © Union Pictures 1994
Recipes © The Contributors 1994
Foreword © Loyd Grossman 1994
Introduction © Richard Bryan 1994
Photographs © Jess Koppel/BBC Enterprises Ltd 1994
Front cover photograph © Random House (UK) Ltd 1994
Back cover photograph © Union Pictures 1994

First published in the United Kingdom in 1994 by Vermilion
an imprint of Ebury Press, Random House, 20 Vauxhall Bridge Road, London SW1V 2SA

Random House Australia (Pty) Limited
20 Alfred Street, Milsons Point, Sydney,
New South Wales 2061, Australia

Random House New Zealand Limited
18 Poland Road, Glenfield
Auckland 10, New Zealand

Random House South Africa (Pty) Limited
PO BOX 337, Bergvlei, South Africa

Random House UK Limited Reg. No. 954009

A CIP catalogue record for this book is available from the British Library

ISBN: 0 09 178686 X

MasterChef 1994
A Union Pictures production for BBC North
Series devised by Franc Roddam
Executive Producers: Bradley Adams and Richard Kalms
Producer and Director: Richard Bryan
Associate Producer: Glynis Robertson
Production Co-ordinators: Louise Brudenell-Bruce and Melanie Jappy

General Editor: Janet Illsley
Design: Clive Dorman
Front cover photograph: Ken Field
Inside photographs: Jess Koppel
Food Stylists: Lyn Rutherford/Mandy Wagstaff
Photographic Stylist: Helen Payne

Typeset by Clive Dorman & Co.
Printed and bound in Great Britain by Clays Limited, St Ives plc.

Papers used by Ebury Press are natural recyclable products made from wood
grown in sustainable forests.

CONTENTS

FOREWORD

Many people are familiar with some form of the quote 'Tell me what you eat and I will tell you who you are' though perhaps fewer will be able to name its author, Jean Anthelme Brillat Savarin, a Napoleonic era lawyer, bureaucrat and gastronome, who is honoured by having various dishes named after him – ranging from eggs to flans to a sautéed woodcock. A still memorable but less famous quote comes from Somerset Maugham, who observed that to eat well in this country meant ordering breakfast three times a day. Put the two quotes together and you may draw the conclusion that the British nation is built out of bacon, eggs and fried bread! So it's unsurprising that as recently as 1955 a journalist wrote 'The British do really want bad, coarse food' going on to say how a generation was happy to live on 'yellow, stodgy eggs and burnt chips soused in cottonseed oil.' I wouldn't pretend that such horrors don't exist in contemporary Britain, but happily the days when someone could write about them as being a national staple are long gone.

The food revolution has come to Britain and not disappeared: our national eating habits have been changed both for the good and for good. Some commentators have hinted in the past few years that the growing number of books, magazine articles, and radio and television programmes are just part of a passing fancy and that some new trend will arrive to take the place of food. I can only cry 'Fiddlesticks!' although maybe 'Sausages!' would be more appropriate. More and more people in Britain are discovering that good food is an important, amusing and enhancing part of everyday life. It is not just for impressing the neighbours or celebrating a birthday: good food is something that we all deserve. And good food, of course, can be something as simple as a sandwich or as elaborate as you fancy.

MasterChef is viewed by more people than any other food programme in British television history and I hope that many of the millions of people who watch will be inspired, stimulated and entertained by what they see being cooked in our now famous red, yellow and blue kitchens. If Somerset Maugham were alive today, I hope that he'd observe that to eat well in Britain you merely have to eat breakfast, lunch or dinner.

Cooking can be an individual or a group activity; television is unquestionably a cooperative pursuit. I am ever grateful to our big and splendid team of cameramen, sound engineers, sparks, runners and washersup. I would most like to thank our indispensible floor manager, Fizz Waters, and all my colleagues at Union Pictures – Franc Roddam, Bradley Adams, Richard Bryan, Glynis Robertson and Melanie Jappy – for their hard work, talent and humour.

Loyd Grossman

Notes for Recipe Users

Quantities are given in metric and imperial measures.
Follow one set of measurements only, not a combination,
because they are not interchangeable.

All spoon measures are level.

Fresh herbs are used unless otherwise stated.

Size 2 eggs are used unless otherwise suggested.

Ovens must be preheated to the temperature
specified in the recipe.

All recipes serve 4.

Front cover photograph: Salad of Griddled Scallops
with Sesame Croûtons and a Walnut Dressing (see page 75)

INTRODUCTION

The champagne corks have come to rest, the television crew have put away their forks and Gerry Goldwyre, our new 1994 MasterChef, has sped home to his magnificent converted water tower outside Edinburgh to recover. Another year of MasterChef is over.

I received a phone call after the last series from a viewer who asked me to impose a rule so that, in future, there would be less puddings based on poached pears. She had a point; ten of the thirty-nine desserts had involved pears. But 1 explained that all the contestants had total freedom to choose their menus provided they adhered to the £30 budget limit and could cook the meal in the allotted two-and-a-half hours.

There are, though, very definitely 'favourite ingredients' each year. 1991 was the year of the lamb, 1992 starred venison and balsamic vinegar, 1993 featured pork and wild mushrooms as well as those pears, and this year game has proved the popular choice. You'll find scrumptious recipes for pigeon and guinea fowl, for pheasant, rabbit and duck, and a couple for that star of yesteryear, venison. But if you are not a meat eater, don't fret. More than a quarter of the main dishes were fish or vegetarian, and as for the puddings, it would be hard to imagine a more luscious or varied selection.

Now it's your turn to enjoy the tasting. We hope that you have as much fun preparing these delicious recipes at home as our contestants have had creating them in the red, yellow and blue kitchens.

RICHARD BRYAN
Producer and Director
MasterChef

—— THE SOUTH WEST & WALES ——

ROGER HEMMING • LYNDA JONES • CHRIS MATTHEWS

PANEL OF JUDGES

Anton Mosimann • Diana Rigg • Loyd Grossman

WINNER

ROGER HEMMING'S MENU

STARTER

Consommé of Shiitake Mushrooms

"That consommé was peerless" **Diana Rigg**

MAIN COURSE

*Fillets of John Dory with a Butter Sauce
perfumed with Cardamom*

Turrets of Wild Rice

Herb-stuffed Cherry Tomatoes

Glazed Fine Green Beans

DESSERT

*Dark Chocolate Horns filled with
a White Chocolate Mousse*

———

Roger Hemming lives in Wellington in Somerset. A former mechanic in the RAF, Roger now manages a successful estate agency in nearby Taunton. His business acumen is also used to full advantage by the Wellington Round Table, for whom he plays an important role in many of the fund-raising events. When he gets time to relax Roger and his wife, Sarah, enjoy walking.

CONSOMMÉ OF SHIITAKE MUSHROOMS

125 g (4 oz) shiitake mushrooms
125 g (4 oz) cultivated button mushrooms
1.2 litres (2 pints) light chicken stock
3 egg whites
salt and freshly ground black pepper
4 flat-leaf parsley sprigs, to garnish

Set aside 4 good shiitake mushrooms for the garnish. Finely chop the rest, along with the button mushrooms.

Bring the chicken stock to a simmer in a saucepan. Add the chopped mushrooms, cover and simmer for 12 to 15 minutes. Strain the flavoured stock and discard the cooked mushroom pulp. Allow the stock to cool briefly.

Beat the egg whites in a bowl until beginning to foam, then whisk into the cooled stock. Continue whisking until a good foamy 'head' appears on the surface.

Return the stock to a gentle heat and slowly bring to a simmer, stirring continuously. Let the consommé simmer gently for 30 minutes. As the egg whites cook, they rise to the surface, drawing up any impurities. At the end of cooking, a solid crust will have formed on the surface, leaving the stock below sparkling and clear. Make a hole in the crust with a ladle, remove from the heat and leave to rest for a few minutes. Pour the clear stock through a jelly bag or a muslin-lined fine sieve.

Remove the stalks from the remaining shiitake mushrooms and finely slice the caps. Place in a small saucepan, moisten with a little of the consommé and cook over a low heat for no more than 30 seconds. Divide the mushroom slices between 4 warmed soup bowls.

Reheat the consommé thoroughly, but do not allow to boil. Check the seasoning, then pour into the soup bowls, allowing the sliced mushrooms to float in the consommé. Serve immediately, garnished with parsley.

Fillets of John Dory with a Cardamom Butter Sauce

Ask your fishmonger to skin and fillet the fish – to provide 4 fillets. Remember to take the skin and bones for the stock.

1 John Dory, weighing about 1.4 kg (3 lb), filleted

Fish Stock:
25 g (1 oz) butter
fish trimming and bones
2 carrots, chopped
½ leek, chopped
1 stick celery, chopped
½ onion, chopped
1 clove garlic, chopped
½ bottle medium dry white wine
1 bay leaf
parsley sprig
thyme sprig

To Finish Sauce:
10 cardamom pods, crushed
few saffron threads
dash of lemon juice
salt and freshly ground black pepper
40 g (1½ oz) butter, in pieces

To Garnish:
¼ green pepper, cored, seeded and finely sliced
8 chives

First make the fish stock. Heat the butter in a wide pan and add the fish trimmings, with the chopped vegetables, garlic and herbs. Cover and sweat over a low heat until the vegetables are softened. Add the wine, herbs and 900 ml (1½ pints) water. Bring to the boil, then simmer until the stock is reduced by two thirds. Strain the stock and return to the pan.

Carefully add the fish fillets to the stock and poach gently for 10 minutes or until just cooked through. Lift out and keep warm in a covered dish. Add the crushed cardamom pods to the pan, with the saffron and a little lemon juice to lift the flavour. Reduce slightly, season to taste with salt and pepper, then whisk in the butter. Strain through a fine sieve.

Divide the sauce equally between 4 warmed serving plates and arrange the fish fillets on top. Garnish with fine slices of green pepper and chives. Serve immediately.

Turrets of Wild Rice

Packets of mixed brown and wild rice are available from larger supermarkets.

350 g (12 oz) mixed brown rice and wild rice
salt
15 g (½ oz) butter
20 ml (4 tsp) fish stock

Cook the rice in boiling salted water for 20 minutes or until just tender. Drain thoroughly. Liberally butter 4 ramekins and divide the rice equally between them. Moisten each one with a little fish stock and cover the tops with foil.

Stand in a roasting tin and pour in just enough water to come halfway up the sides of the ramekins. Bake in a preheated oven at 200°C (400°F) mark 6 for 8-10 minutes. Take out of the roasting tin, remove the foil and invert a warmed serving plate over each ramekin. Turn the right way up and shake gently to release each turret of rice. Serve at once.

HERB-STUFFED CHERRY TOMATOES

8 firm cherry tomatoes
300 ml (½ pint) single cream
salt and freshly ground black pepper
10 ml (2 tsp) chopped parsley
30 ml (2 tbsp) fine white breadcrumbs
basil leaves, to garnish

Using a sharp knife, slit the skin of the tomatoes. Plunge into a bowl of boiling water for 2-5 seconds to loosen the skins. Refresh in cold water, then remove the skins – they should now slip off easily. Cut off the top of each tomato, carefully scoop out the seeds and discard.

Pour the single cream into a pan, heat to boiling point and simmer to gently reduce by half. Remove from the heat. Season with salt and pepper and add the chopped parsley.

Carefully fill each tomato with the cream and parsley mixture whilst still warm. The heat will warm the tomatoes through without causing them to lose shape. Sprinkle the breadcrumbs over the tops of the tomatoes, flash under a hot grill for a few seconds to brown, then serve immediately, garnished with basil leaves.

GLAZED FINE GREEN BEANS

300 g (10 oz) fine green beans
22 g (¾ oz) butter
salt and freshly ground black pepper

Top and tail the beans. Cook, uncovered, in plenty of boiling salted water for 2 minutes; the beans should still be firm at this stage. Remove and refresh in cold water. (This stage can be done in advance.)

To serve, melt the butter in a pan with 45 ml (3 tbsp) water, a twist of pepper and a pinch of salt. Add the beans and cook for 1 minute. Check the seasoning and serve immediately.

DARK CHOCOLATE HORNS FILLED WITH A WHITE CHOCOLATE MOUSSE

Chocolate Horns:
225 g (8 oz) quality dark chocolate

White Chocolate Mousse:
50 g (2 oz) quality white chocolate
30 ml (2 tbsp) Browns liqueur Muscat
1 egg, separated
75 ml (2½ fl oz) double cream
2.5 ml (½ tsp) powdered gelatine
10 ml (2 tsp) milk

Apricot Sauce:
200 ml (7 oz) dried apricots
120 ml (4 fl oz) water
50 g (2 oz) caster sugar
15 ml (1 tbsp) lemon juice, or to taste
15 ml (1 tbsp) Browns liqueur Muscat

To make the chocolate horns, carefully line 8 cream horn tins with non-stick baking parchment. Break the chocolate into pieces and place in a bowl standing over a pan of hot (recently boiled) water until melted. Stir until smooth. Using a clean pastry brush, apply an even coating of chocolate to the inside of each lined tin, making sure that there are no holes and that the chocolate reaches the top of the horn. Chill until set. Pipe any remaining chocolate into abstract shapes on a piece of non-stick baking parchment to use for decoration. Chill until set.

Gently remove the horns from the moulds, peel away the paper and leave in the refrigerator until needed.

To prepare the white chocolate mousse, break the chocolate into pieces and place in a heatproof bowl over a pan of hot (recently boiled) water. As the chocolate melts, incorporate the Muscat liqueur and 15 ml (1 tbsp) luke-warm water. Stir until smooth and evenly blended. Lightly beat the egg yolk and stir into the mixture.

Whip the double cream in a bowl until it just holds its shape. Carefully fold into the chocolate mixture. Soften the gelatine in the milk, then place the bowl over a pan of simmering water until the gelatine is dissolved. Stir into the chocolate mixture and chill the mixture until it begins to thicken.

Whisk the egg white until stiff, then fold gently into the chocolate mousse mixture. Leave until thickened to the consistency of whipped cream. Fill the chocolate horns with the mousse and chill for 1 hour before serving.

To make the apricot sauce, put the dried apricots in a saucepan with the water, sugar and lemon juice. Simmer for 20 minutes until the apricots begin to break up and form a syrup. Cool slightly, then purée in a food processor or blender. Pass through a sieve to ensure a smooth result. Add the muscat liqueur and adjust the flavour with more lemon juice if necessary. Chill in the refrigerator until required.

To serve, pool the apricot sauce on individual serving plates and arrange the chocolate horns on top. Decorate with the chocolate shapes and serve immediately.

Note: Avoid overhandling the chocolate horns as they are easily spoilt by finger prints. Chocolate-dipped Cape goose-berries also make a pretty decoration.

——THE SOUTH WEST & WALES——

ROGER HEMMING • LYNDA JONES • CHRIS MATTHEWS

PANEL OF JUDGES

Anton Mosimann • Diana Rigg • Loyd Grossman

LYNDA JONES' MENU

STARTER

*Roulades of Lemon Sole and Lobster Mousseline,
served with a Lemon and Lime Butter Sauce*

MAIN COURSE

Noisettes of Welsh Lamb with a Bramble Sauce

Potato Rösti

Baby Vegetables

DESSERT

*Strawberry Shortbread Surprise,
served with a Strawberry Coulis*

"The pudding was absolutely delicious...light and good" **Diana Rigg**

———

L ynda Jones and her family from Lampeter in Dyfed are sheep and cattle farmers. Lynda's many tasks including rounding up the pedigree sheep with the aid of her dog, and bidding at the local cattle auctions. She is the only young farmer in Britain to have gained seven of the Young Farmers Gold Craft Certificates.

ROULADES OF LEMON SOLE AND LOBSTER MOUSSELINE

Ask your fishmonger to fillet and skin the lemon sole for you – to provide 4 fillets.

2 lemon sole, filleted and skinned
175 g (6 oz) cooked lobster meat
½ egg white (size 2)
150 ml (¼ pint) whipping cream
salt and freshly ground black pepper

Lemon and Lime Butter Sauce:
¼ shallot, finely diced
12 black peppercorns, crushed
60 ml (4 tbsp) white wine
30 ml (2 tbsp) lemon juice
30 ml (2 tbsp) lime juice
100 ml (3½ fl oz) vegetable stock
100 g (4 oz) unsalted butter, chilled and
   diced

To Garnish:
snipped chives
cooked lobster claws (optional)

To make the roulade, place the lobster meat in a food processor and purée for a few seconds only. Add the egg white through the feeder tube, processing briefly until smooth and firm. Pass the mixture through a fine sieve into a bowl. Stand the bowl over some ice, then add the cream, a little at a time, mixing thoroughly after each addition. Season with salt and pepper to taste and chill in the refrigerator for about 20 minutes.

Meanwhile, make the lemon and lime sauce. Place the shallot, peppercorns, wine, lemon and lime juices in a small pan and reduce. Add the vegetable stock and reduce again. Gradually work in the chilled butter a piece at a time, whisking constantly on and off the heat, but do not allow to boil again.

Lay each sole fillet, skin-side down, on a piece of greaseproof paper or non-stick baking parchment. Season lightly, then cover each fillet with lobster mousseline. Roll up the fillets, to enclose the filling. Wrap the paper around each roulade, securing the edges and ends firmly to ensure the fish is well sealed.

To cook, place the sole roulades in a steamer over gently boiling water and steam for 4-5 minutes or until the mousseline has turned pink and is firm to the touch. Allow to rest for a few minutes before serving.

To serve, carefully reheat the sauce. Unwrap the roulades and cut each one into slices. Arrange on warmed serving plates and pour the sauce around them. Sprinkle with the snipped chives and garnish with lobster claws if available. Serve at once.

NOISETTES OF WELSH LAMB WITH A BRAMBLE SAUCE

Ask your butcher to bone the lamb for you. Use the bones and trimmings to prepare a well-flavoured lamb stock.

1.1 kg (2½ lb) best end of lamb, boned
salt and freshly ground black pepper
30 ml (2 tbsp) olive oil

Sauce:
600 ml (1 pint) homemade lamb stock
150 ml (¼ pint) dry white wine
15 ml (1 tbsp) bramble jelly
squeeze of lemon juice
1 mint sprig
10-15 ml (2-3 tsp) brandy
knob of butter
about 5 ml (1 tsp) arrowroot (optional)

To Garnish:
rosemary sprigs

Trim the lamb if necessary and season with salt and pepper.

To make the bramble sauce, pour the stock into a saucepan and boil steadily until reduced by half. Add the wine and reduce by one third. Add the bramble jelly, seasoning, lemon juice and mint. Reduce slightly. Add the brandy and butter. If the sauce requires thickening, blend the arrowroot with a little water, stir into the sauce and cook, stirring, for 1 minute until thickened and clear.

To cook the lamb, heat the oil in a frying pan and quickly seal the lamb on all sides. Transfer to a roasting tin and cook in a preheated oven at 230°C (450°F) mark 8 for 17 minutes. Wrap in foil and leave to rest in a warm place for a few minutes.

To serve, carve the lamb into thick slices and arrange on warmed serving plates. Garnish with rosemary and serve with the rösti and baby vegetables.

POTATO RÖSTI

800 g (1¾ lb) potatoes
salt and freshly ground black pepper
freshly grated nutmeg
50 g (2 oz) butter

Peel the potatoes, then grate coarsely, using a food processor grating disc if possible. Season with salt, pepper and nutmeg to taste.

Melt the butter in a frying pan. Place heaped spoonfuls of the potato in the frying pan and shape into flat round cakes. Cook on a moderate heat for a few minutes until crisp and golden underneath, then turn and fry the other side until cooked. Drain on kitchen paper and serve at once.

BABY VEGETABLES

10 baby corn cobs
20 baby carrots
2 cauliflower florets, divided into small
  sprigs
4 broccoli florets, divided into small sprigs
20 mangetouts
50 g (2 oz) butter

Bring a pan of salted water to the boil. Add the baby corn and carrots and simmer for 5 minutes. Add the cauliflower and cook for a further 3 minutes. Finally add the broccoli and mangetouts and cook for 1 minute. Drain the vegetables thoroughly. Put the butter in the warm pan to melt. Add the vegetables and turn to coat in the butter. Serve at once.

STRAWBERRY SHORTBREAD SURPRISE, WITH A STRAWBERRY COULIS

Strawberry Surprise:
30 ml (2 tbsp) water
7 g (¼ oz) gelatine
125 g (4 oz) soft cream cheese
1 egg (size 2)
75 ml (5 tbsp) double cream
30 ml (2 tbsp) strawberry conserve
30 ml (2 tbsp) kirsch

Shortbread:
125 g (4½ oz) plain white flour
pinch of salt
90 g (3½ oz) unsalted butter, diced
50 g (2 oz) icing sugar
1 egg yolk
few drops of vanilla essence
beaten egg, to glaze

Strawberry Coulis:
225 g (8 oz) strawberries
40 g (1½ oz) sugar
few drops of lemon juice

To Decorate:
icing sugar, for dusting
a little double cream
few strawberries, sliced

To make the strawberry surprise, put the water in a bowl, sprinkle on the gelatine and leave to soften and swell. In a bowl, whisk the cream cheese, egg yolk, cream, strawberry conserve and kirsch together until light and fluffy. Stand the bowl of gelatine in a pan of hot water until dissolved, then whisk the dissolved gelatine into the cheese mixture. Whisk the egg white in another bowl until soft peaks form, then fold into the mixture.

Divide between 4 individual moulds, about 6 cm (2½ inches) in diameter and 4 cm (1½ inches) in depth (see note). Chill in the refrigerator until set.

To make the shortbread, sift the flour and salt into a bowl and make a well in the centre. Add the butter to the well and work it until very soft. Add the icing sugar and mix into the butter, then add the egg yolk and vanilla essence. Gradually draw in the flour and mix thoroughly to a smooth dough. Wrap in cling film and leave to rest in the refrigerator for 20 minutes.

Roll out the shortbread dough on a lightly floured surface and cut out five or six 6 cm (2½ inch) rounds, using a pastry cutter. Stamp out small hearts from the remaining dough, using a heart-shaped cutter. Place on a baking sheet. Brush the heart-shaped biscuits with beaten egg. Bake the shortbread in a preheated oven at 200°C (400°F) mark 6 for 6-8 minutes until light golden in colour. Transfer to a wire rack to cool.

To make the strawberry coulis, put the strawberries, sugar and lemon juice in a saucepan and heat gently until the sugar is dissolved. Immediately remove from the heat and purée in a blender or food processor. Pass through a fine sieve to remove the pips.

To serve, cover each plate with a pool of strawberry coulis. To unmould each strawberry surprise, wrap a hot tea-towel around the mould, then invert onto a shortbread round. Position in the middle of the coulis. Dust the heart-shaped biscuits with icing sugar and position on the edge of the plate. Place dots of cream on the coulis and feather with a skewer. Decorate with strawberry slices and serve at once.

Note: To set the mousses, you can use individual rings placed on a flat tray if moulds are unavailable. The shortbread recipe makes a few more biscuits than required, to allow for breakages.

THE SOUTH WEST & WALES

ROGER HEMMING • LYNDA JONES • CHRIS MATTHEWS

PANEL OF JUDGES
Anton Mosimann • Diana Rigg • Loyd Grossman

CHRIS MATTHEWS' MENU

STARTER

Tarragon Mousse with Potato and Horseradish Galettes,
served with Salad Leaves in a Herb Vinaigrette

"Excellent Idea" **Anton Mosimann**

MAIN COURSE

Breast of Pheasant en Papillote
with Kumquats and a Port and Madeira Sauce

Quenelles of Onion and Grenadine

Rosettes of Three Cabbages

DESSERT

Caramelised Puff Pastry Boxes
filled with Muscovado Apples and Cinnamon Cream,
served with a Caramel and Calvados Sauce

Chris Matthews, from Clifton near Bristol, is a graphic designer and has been running his own small company for several years. Chris has a passion for elephants, and spends many an hour with his nephew and niece and a bag of apples visiting Wendy, Bristol Zoo's splendid African elephant! The long winter evenings find Chris hard at work building scale model racing cars, another of his passions.

TARRAGON MOUSSE WITH POTATO AND HORSERADISH GALETTES

Tarragon Mousse:
125 g (4 oz) skinless chicken breast fillet, roughly chopped
1 egg white
200 ml (7 fl oz) double cream
coarse sea salt and freshly ground black pepper
4 tarragon sprigs
600 ml (1 pint) chicken stock

Potato and Horseradish Galettes:
150 g (5 oz) potato, finely grated
40 g (1½ oz) horseradish, finely grated
pinch of salt
15 g (½ oz) unsalted butter, melted

To Serve:
50 g (2 oz) lamb fillet
Salad Leaves in Herb Vinaigrette (see right)
tarragon sprigs, to garnish

To make the tarragon mousse, put the chicken breast in a blender or food processor and work to a purée. With the motor running, add the egg white through the feeder tube and process briefly until the mixture thickens. Add the cream slowly in the same way. Season liberally with salt and pepper. Transfer to a bowl. Finely chop the tarragon and stir into the mousse mixture. Cover and chill in the refrigerator until needed.

To make the galettes, wrap the grated potato in a tea towel and squeeze to extract all excess moisture. Turn into a mixing bowl and add the horseradish and salt; stir well. Add the melted butter and toss well. Divide the mixture into eight portions. Position a 7.5 cm (3 inch) metal ring mould on a lightly buttered baking sheet and spread a portion of the mixture in the ring. Remove the ring and repeat to make eight galettes in

total. Bake in a preheated oven at 200°C (400°F) mark 6 for about 10 minutes until golden on both sides, turning the galettes halfway through cooking.

To cook the mousses, pour the chicken stock into a small frying pan and set four buttered 6 cm (2½ inch) metal ring moulds in the pan. Fill the moulds with the mousse mixture and cook over a moderate heat for about 10 minutes, until firm to the touch. Set pan aside in a warm place until ready to serve.

Meanwhile cut the lamb fillet into four thin slices and flash-fry in a dry heavy-based non-stick frying pan on both sides until browned.

Season each galette with one twist of the salt mill. Position one galette in the centre of each warmed serving plate and place a mousse on top. Add a slice of lamb and top with the remaining galettes. Surround with the dressed salad leaves. Garnish with tarragon leaves and serve immediately.

Note: The galettes can be prepared and cooked in advance; warm through in the oven for 5 minutes before serving.

SALAD LEAVES IN A HERB VINAIGRETTE

about 100 g (3½ oz) endive (frisée or batavia)
about 100 g (3½ oz) radicchio leaves

Herb Vinaigrette:
75 ml (5 tbsp) olive oil
1 shallot, crushed
1 thyme sprig
1 basil leaf
4 rosemary sprig needles
1 chervil sprig
15 ml (1 tbsp) white wine vinegar
45 ml (3 tbsp) cold water
1.25 ml (¼ tsp) salt
1.25 ml (¼ tsp) white pepper
1.25 ml (¼ tsp) caster sugar

To make the herb vinaigrette, combine the olive oil, shallot and herbs together in a small saucepan. Bring to a simmer, then remove from the heat. Leave to stand for 2 hours. Strain the mixture through a fine sieve into a bowl. Whisk in the vinegar, water, salt, pepper and sugar.

Just before serving, toss the salad leaves in the dressing.

BREAST OF PHEASANT EN PAPILLOTE WITH KUMQUATS AND A PORT AND MADEIRA SAUCE

4 skinless pheasant breast fillets
8 juniper berries
4 thyme sprigs
a little white wine
salt and freshly ground black pepper

Port and Madeira Sauce:
15 ml (1 tbsp) sunflower oil
125 g (4 oz) button mushrooms, finely chopped
15 g (½ oz) unsalted butter
6 shallots, finely chopped
60 ml (2 fl oz) sherry vinegar
60 ml (2 fl oz) port
60 ml (2 fl oz) Madeira
200 ml (7 fl oz) veal stock
90 ml (3 fl oz) chicken stock
15 ml (1 tbsp) whipping cream
1 thyme sprig
1 strip of orange rind

To Garnish:
4 kumquats, thinly sliced
4 watercress sprigs

To cook the pheasant, butter four 15 x 20 cm (6 x 8 inch) pieces of foil and place a pheasant breast in the centre of each. Lightly crush the juniper berries and sprinkle over the meat. Place a sprig of thyme on each pheasant breast and moisten with a little white wine. Season with salt and pepper and fold the foil to enclose the meat and make neat papillotes. Bake in a preheated oven at 200°C (400°F) mark 6 for 15 minutes.

Meanwhile make the port and madeira sauce. Heat the oil in a pan, add the mushrooms and sauté for 2-3 minutes; set aside.

Heat the butter in a small saucepan, add the shallots and allow to sweat until they turn reddish-brown. Deglaze with the sherry vinegar. When the liquid has evaporated, add the port and Madeira, then add the sautéed mushrooms. Cook over moderate heat until reduced by two-thirds, skimming occasionally. Stir in the veal stock, chicken stock and whipping cream, then add the thyme and orange rind. Bring to the boil and skim. Pass the sauce through a fine sieve into a small saucepan; there should be about 250 ml (8 fl oz).

To serve, unwrap the papillotes and diagonally slice the pheasant breasts. Divide the sauce evenly between the warmed serving plates and arrange the pheasant slices on top. Garnish with the kumquats and watercress sprigs. Serve at once, with the quenelles of onion and rosettes of cabbage.

QUENELLES OF ONION AND GRENADINE

15 ml (1 tbsp) oil
15 g (½ oz) unsalted butter
250 g (9 oz) onions, finely chopped
15 ml (1 tbsp) red wine vinegar
30 ml (2 tbsp) red wine
90 ml (3 fl oz) grenadine
15 ml (1 tbsp) Sauternes

Heat the oil and butter in a pan, add the onions and sweat gently until transparent. Add the red wine vinegar and red wine and reduce over a moderate heat. Add the grenadine and Sauternes and reduce until the liquid has completely evaporated and the onions are soft. Shape the mixture into quenelles. Serve piping hot.

ROSETTES OF THREE CABBAGES

Braised Red Cabbage:
10 ml (2 tsp) duck fat
¼ onion, finely chopped
10 ml (2 tsp) caster sugar
½ red cabbage, cored and sliced
30 ml (2 tbsp) red wine vinegar
120 ml (4 fl oz) chicken stock
2 pinches each of ground cinnamon, ground
  cloves and ground allspice

Braised White Cabbage:
15 ml (1 tbsp) duck fat
¼ white cabbage, cored and sliced
3 juniper berries, lightly crushed
30 ml (2 tbsp) white wine
salt and freshly ground black pepper

Brussels Sprouts:
knob of unsalted butter
4 Brussels sprouts, finely sliced
12 hazelnuts, roughly chopped

To prepare the braised red cabbage, heat the duck fat in a heavy-based pan and sauté the onion until transparent. Add the caster sugar and red cabbage and stir well. Add the red wine vinegar and allow to reduce. Add the chicken stock and spices. Stir, then cover and braise for about 1 hour until tender.

For the braised white cabbage, heat the duck fat in a heavy-based pan, add the white cabbage, juniper berries, white wine and seasoning. Stir well, cover and braise for about 30 minutes until tender.

For the Brussels sprouts, heat the butter in a small sauté pan until sizzling. Add the Brussels sprouts and sauté for 2-3 minutes. Add the hazelnuts and heat through; keep warm.

To assemble, place a small mound of Brussels sprouts on each warmed side plate. Surround with concentric circles of white, and then red cabbage. Serve immediately.

CARAMELISED PUFF PASTRY BOXES FILLED WITH MUSCOVADO APPLES AND CINNAMON CREAM

225 g (8 oz) puff pastry
icing sugar, for dredging
50 g (2 oz) caster sugar
3 cooking apples
juice of ½ lemon
250 ml (8 fl oz) sunflower oil
225 g (8 oz) dark muscovado sugar
300 ml (½ pint) whipping cream
a little ground cinnamon

Caramel and Calvados Sauce:
60 ml (2 fl oz) cold water
250 g (9 oz) caster sugar
150 ml (¼ pint) hot water
30 ml (2 tbsp) Calvados

To Decorate:
12 redcurrants
1 eating apple, thinly sliced
4 blackberries
4 mint sprigs

Roll out the puff pastry thinly on a lightly floured surface to a rectangle, measuring about 33 x 25 cm (13 x 10 inches) and cut out twenty 6 cm (2½ inch) squares. Place on a board, cover and chill in the refrigerator for 20-30 minutes. Prick the pastry squares with a fork and place on a large baking sheet. Cover with another baking sheet and weigh down with some medium (not heavy) weights to stop the pastry rising. Place in a preheated oven at 220°C (425°F) mark 7. Turn the oven down to 200°C (400°F) mark 6 and bake for 7-8 minutes. Remove the weights and the top tray and bake the pastry squares for a further 5-6 minutes, or until golden. Transfer to a wire rack to cool.

Sift icing sugar liberally over the pastry squares, making sure each square is well covered, then place under a hot grill for about 30-40 seconds to caramelise the sugar. Allow to cool.

To make the caramel and calvados sauce, put the cold water in a small heavy-based pan. Add the caster sugar, forming a mound in the centre of the pan. Dissolve over a low heat, then bring to the boil. Cook the syrup over a medium heat until it is a rich caramel colour. When the caramel develops a slightly bitter aroma immediately remove from the heat. Tilt the pan away from you and add the hot water. (Be careful, as this will cause the caramel to spit for a few seconds.) Return to the heat and simmer for 1 minute, then remove and let cool. When cool, add the Calvados. Set aside.

To make the boxes, melt the caster sugar in a heavy-based pan over a low heat. Carefully dip one side of a pastry square into the melted sugar, then press against another square at a 90° angle; this forms two sides of the box. Continue in this way to make the third and fourth sides. Repeat to make 4 boxes in total. (The remaining squares will be lids.)

Peel the cooking apples and scoop the flesh into balls, with a small melon baller. Immerse in a bowl of water acidulated with the lemon juice for 2-3 minutes. Heat the oil in a heavy-based saucepan. Drain the apples and pat dry with kitchen paper. Dredge the apple balls with muscovado sugar and fry in the hot oil for 1 minute. Remove with a slotted spoon and allow to cool.

Whip the cream until thick and flavour with cinnamon to taste. Place a caramelised pastry box on each serving plate and half fill with apple balls. Top with the cinnamon cream and redcurrants, then place a lid at an angle on top. Pour the caramel and calvados sauce around the boxes. Decorate with the apple slices, blackberries and mint. Serve immediately.

THE HOME COUNTIES
ALISON FIANDER • SARA DOUGLAS • CHRIS RAND

PANEL OF JUDGES
Michel Roux Jnr • Carol Thatcher • Loyd Grossman

WINNER

ALISON FIANDER'S MENU

STARTER
*Seafood Parcels
with a Chive and Lemon Sauce*
"That's terrifically good" **Loyd**

MAIN COURSE
*Lamb with Pumpkin Risotto
Chicory and Watercress Salad*

DESSERT
Raspberry Surprise
"Extremely delicious pudding" **Loyd**

A lison Fiander, from new Malden in Surrey, is a Special Events Manager which demands creativity and considerable energy. Alison's creative talents are also evident in her impressive hobbies, water colour painting and intricate embroidery.

SEAFOOD PARCELS WITH A CHIVE AND LEMON SAUCE

50 g (2 oz) bean sprouts
50 g (2 oz) shelled queen scallops
50 g (2 oz) cooked peeled prawns
5 ml (1 tsp) grated fresh root ginger
30 ml (2 tbsp) chopped coriander leaves
salt and freshly ground black pepper
8 sheets filo pastry (maximum – see note)
about 50 g (2 oz) butter, melted

Chive and Lemon Sauce:
50 g (2 oz) butter
15 ml (1 tbsp) lemon juice
15 ml (1 tbsp) chopped chives

Blanch the bean sprouts for 30 seconds in boiling water; drain. Blanch the scallops in boiling water for 30 seconds; drain.

In a bowl, combine the prawns, scallops, bean sprouts, grated ginger and chopped coriander leaves. Season with salt and pepper to taste.

To make the parcels, take one sheet of filo pastry and brush it with melted butter. Top with a second sheet of filo and brush again with melted butter. Cut out a 15 x 10 cm (6 x 4 inch) 'double' rectangle. With the long side towards you, place an eighth of the filling in a sausage shape across the centre. Fold in the short sides over the filling, brushing them with a little melted butter, then roll up the parcel to completely enclose the filling. Repeat with the remaining filo and filling to make 8 parcels in total.

Place the parcels seam-side down on a greased baking sheet and brush with melted butter. Bake in a preheated oven at 230°C (450°F) mark 8 for 8-10 minutes, or until golden brown and crisp. To make the sauce, melt the butter, then whisk in the lemon juice and chives. Drizzle the sauce over the parcels to serve.

Note: If the filo sheets you buy are large ones, you won't need as many.

LAMB WITH PUMPKIN RISOTTO

I prefer to use organic meat, which I buy from The Real Meat Company.

450 g (1 lb) boned loin of lamb
coarse sea salt and freshly ground black
    pepper
30 ml (2 tbsp) extra-virgin olive oil
45-60 ml (3-4 tbsp) red or white wine
45-60 ml (3-4 tbsp) lamb stock

Pumpkin Risotto:
90 ml (6 tbsp) extra-virgin olive oil
2 onions, chopped
2 cloves garlic, chopped
2 large red chillis, deseeded and chopped
300 g (10 oz) Arborio rice
250 ml (8 fl oz) white wine (eg Australian
    Semilion Chardonnay)
5 ml (1 tsp) turmeric
about 1.2 litres (2 pints) chicken stock
250 g (9 oz) butternut squash or pumpkin,
    finely chopped
100 g (3½ oz) goat's cheese, cut into small
    pieces
100 g (3½ oz) pine nuts, toasted

First prepare the risotto. Heat the olive oil in a frying pan, add the onions and garlic and fry until softened. Stir in the chopped chillis. Add the rice and cook for 2-3 minutes, then add the wine and stir gently until the liquid is absorbed. Stir in the turmeric.

Gradually start adding the chicken stock, stirring constantly over a low heat. Continue adding the stock, a ladleful at a time, as each addition is absorbed. Once half the stock has been absorbed, add the pumpkin. Continue to stir in the stock until the rice is plump and tender but still retains a bite. The maximum cooking time is 30 minutes; you may not need to use all of the stock.

When the risotto is nearly ready, cook the lamb. Season the meat with the pepper. Heat the oil in a frying pan, add the lamb and fry over a very high heat for 2-3 minutes each side. Transfer to a warmed dish and allow to stand briefly before carving. Meanwhile, deglaze the pan with the wine and stock, stirring to scrape up the sediment.

When the risotto is cooked, stir in the goat's cheese, turn off the heat and cover the pan to encourage the cheese to melt.

To serve, season the meat with salt and pepper and slice thinly. Fold most of the pine nuts into the risotto. Spoon the risotto onto warmed serving plates and arrange the lamb slices alongside. Moisten the meat with a little of the deglazed pan juices. Sprinkle the remaining pine nuts over the risotto and serve at once, accompanied by the chicory and watercress salad.

CHICORY AND WATERCRESS SALAD

1 bunch of watercress
2 heads of chicory

Vinaigrette:
15 ml (1 tbsp) tarragon vinegar
45 ml (3 tbsp) walnut oil
salt and freshly ground black pepper

Trim the watercress; rinse and drain thoroughly. Separate the chicory leaves. Put the watercress and chicory into a bowl.

To make the vinaigrette, put the vinegar and oil in a screw-topped jar with salt and pepper to taste. Shake vigorously to combine.

Pour the dressing over the salad leaves and toss lightly. Serve at once.

RASPBERRY SURPRISE

Whisked Sponge:
50 g (2 oz) plain flour
pinch of salt
2 eggs (size 2)
65 g (2½ oz) caster sugar

Topping:
225 g (8 oz) raspberries (fresh or frozen and defrosted)
300 ml (½ pint) soured cream
75 g (3 oz) caster sugar

To Decorate:
100 g (3½ oz) quality plain dark chocolate
300 ml (½ pint) double cream
5 ml (1 tsp) caster sugar

To make the whisked sponge, line two 15 cm (6 inch) round cake tins with non-stick baking parchment. Sift the flour and salt together; set aside. Put the eggs into a mixing bowl and gradually beat in the sugar. Place the bowl over a saucepan, one third full of boiling water, making sure the bowl does not touch the water. Using an electric hand whisk, whisk the eggs and sugar together until the mixture is thick, light in colour and significantly increased in volume; this will take at least 5 minutes. Remove the bowl from the pan. Lightly fold the flour into the mixture, using a metal spoon.

Divide the mixture between the prepared cake tins. Bake in a preheated oven at 190°C (375°F) mark 5 for about 20 minutes, until well risen and golden brown. Turn out and cool on a wire rack. You will only need to use one of the sponges for this dessert, so freeze the other one for another occasion.

Line four individual 7.5-10 cm (3-4 inch) round tins with non-stick baking parchment. Slice the sponge horizontally into two layers, then cut into smaller pieces and use to cover the base

of the tins. Scatter the raspberries over the sponge, reserving a few for decoration. Stir the soured cream and sugar together, then pour over the raspberries. Bake in a preheated oven at 180°C (350°F) mark 4 for 25 minutes until set. Allow to cool in the tins.

Meanwhile make the chocolate scrolls. Break the chocolate into pieces and place in a small bowl over a pan of hot water until melted. Stir until smooth, then pour onto a clean flat surface, preferably a marble slab, and allow to cool and set. Hold a long-bladed knife in both hands and push the blade away from you along the surface of the chocolate to shave off long scrolls.

To finish, carefully remove the desserts from their tins and place on individual plates. Whip the double cream with the 5 ml (1 tsp) caster sugar and spread over the top of the desserts. Decorate with the dark chocolate scrolls and reserved raspberries.

Note: If individual tins are not available, use a 20 cm (8 inch) loose-bottomed cake tin instead.

THE HOME COUNTIES

ALISON FIANDER • SARA DOUGLAS • CHRIS RAND

PANEL OF JUDGES

Michel Roux Jnr • Carol Thatcher • Loyd Grossman

SARA DOUGLAS' MENU

STARTER

*Ravioli of Goat's Cheese
with Roasted Plum Tomato Sauce*

MAIN COURSE

*Mosaic of Salmon
and Cod with Sorrel Sauce*

"Very Dainty" **Michel Roux Jnr**

Wild Rice

Julienne of Vegetables

DESSERT

Raspberry and Almond Stacks

"The sauce is fantastic. Fruity and not too sweet" **Carol Thatcher**

S ara Douglas, from Cheam in Surrey, is a debt recovery executive for a Russian bank in the city. Working very close to Leadenhall market, Sara takes full advantage of the amazing range of fresh foods available there each day… and counters their effect by rowing and cycling for many miles during lunch time visits to her local health club.

RAVIOLI OF GOAT'S CHEESE WITH ROASTED PLUM TOMATO SAUCE

The best flour to use for this pasta is a very fine-textured wheat flour, known as type '00' – available from Italian delicatessens.

Pasta:
113 g (4 oz) type '00' pasta flour
1 egg (size 2)
1 egg yolk
few drops of olive oil
½ teaspoon salt

Filling:
175 g (6 oz) goat's cheese
20 basil leaves
30 ml (2 tbsp) pine nuts, lightly toasted

Sauce:
6 large plum tomatoes
olive oil, for basting
1 onion, chopped
4 cloves garlic, chopped
6-8 basil sprigs
75 ml (5 tbsp) dry white wine
6 cherry tomatoes
salt and freshly ground black pepper

To Serve:
30 ml (2 tbsp) pine nuts, lightly toasted
basil leaves, to garnish

To make the pasta, put all the ingredients into a food processor. Blend for about 30 seconds until the dough forms a neat ball. Knead on a floured board for about 6-8 minutes until smooth. Wrap the dough in cling film and leave to rest in the refrigerator for about 1 hour.

To prepare the filling, put the goat's cheese and 8 basil leaves into a blender or food processor. Blend for about 40-45 seconds. Turn into a bowl and stir in the pine nuts. Cover and refrigerate.

To make the sauce, halve the plum tomatoes and remove the core. Brush the skins with olive oil, then place the tomatoes in a roasting tin with the onion, garlic and basil. Drizzle olive oil liberally over the tomatoes and add the white wine. Heat through on top of the cooker, then transfer to a preheated oven at 230°C (450°F) mark 8 for about 30 minutes until the tomato skins are blackened. Transfer to a food processor, add the cherry tomatoes and blend for 1-2 minutes. Pass the sauce through a sieve and season with salt and pepper to taste.

To shape the ravioli, cut the dough into 4 portions; re-wrap 3 portions. Flatten the other piece with a rolling pin and put through a pasta machine twice on its widest setting and then twice on each subsequent narrower setting until the pasta is as thin as possible, dusting with a little flour as necessary. Pass through only once on setting 7.

Using a 7.5 cm (3 inch) plain cutter, cut out circles of pasta. Take a rounded teaspoonful of goat's cheese filling and place in the centre of the circle. Lay a basil leaf on top. Fold the pasta over the filling to form a semi-circle and seal the edges carefully with thumb and forefinger, brushing with a little water if necessary. (Ensure that the edges are well sealed.) Repeat to make 12 ravioli in total.

Bring a large pan of water to the boil, with a few drops of olive oil added. Cook the ravioli in batches for 1-2 minutes, refresh briefly in cold water. If not using immediately, brush with oil and place on a baking sheet.

To serve, return the sauce to a pan and heat through. Add the ravioli and heat through. Place 3 ravioli on each warmed serving plate and spoon over the sauce. Sprinkle with the toasted pine nuts and grind over some black pepper. Garnish with basil leaves and serve immediately.

MOSAIC OF SALMON AND COD WITH SORREL SAUCE

2 thick cod fillets, skinned, each about 300 g
    (10 oz)
2 thick salmon fillets, skinned, each about
    225 g (8 oz)
juice of 1 lemon
salt and freshly ground white pepper
16-20 large spinach leaves
Japanese dried seaweed, for steaming
    (optional)

Sorrel Sauce:
225 g (8 oz) sorrel
50 g (2 oz) butter
250 ml (8 fl oz) single cream
250 ml (8 fl oz) double cream
30-45 ml (2-3 tbsp) reduced fish stock
few drops of lemon juice

Trim the top of each fish fillet as necessary, to leave a flat fillet approximately 2 cm (¾ inch) thick. Cut each cod fillet lengthways into 8 strips, each about 10 x 2 x 2 cm (4 x ¾ x ¾ inch) (see note). Cut each salmon fillet widthways into 8 strips, each about 2 cm (¾ inch) wide. Sprinkle with lemon juice and season with salt and white pepper.

Wash the spinach leaves thoroughly and remove the thick stalks. Blanch the spinach in boiling water for 1 minute or so until pliable. Drain thoroughly. Wrap each cod strip in a blanched spinach leaf. Weave four strips of each fish together to form a chequerboard, trimming the salmon as necessary. Season each mosaic well with salt and pepper.

If using seaweed, cover with cold water and leave to soak for 10 minutes, then drain. Half-fill a large frying pan with water and bring to the boil. Take a large steamer and line with the seaweed if using. Lay the fish in the steamer. Set over the frying pan. Cover and steam for about 8-10 minutes until the salmon flakes easily when tested.

Meanwhile prepare the sauce. Wash the sorrel leaves thoroughly and remove the thick stalks. Melt the butter in a saucepan, add the sorrel leaves and cook gently until wilted. In a separate pan, gently heat the creams together, taking care not to allow the mixture to boil. Add the fish stock and sorrel; stir well. Add the lemon juice and season with salt and pepper to taste.

To serve, place a mosaic on each warmed serving plate and pour on some of the sorrel sauce. Hand the extra sorrel sauce separately, in a small jug. Serve immediately, with the wild rice and vegetable julienne.

Note: If it isn't possible to cut 10 cm (4 inch) lengths, wrap shorter pieces together to achieve the required length.

WILD RICE

225 g (8 oz) mixed basmati and wild rice
salt and freshly ground black pepper
½ courgette
15 g (½ oz) unsalted butter
flat-leaved parsley, to garnish

Add the rice to a large pan of salted water. Bring to the boil and simmer, uncovered, for about 18-20 minutes until cooked. Meanwhile trim and coarsely grate the courgette.

Drain the cooked rice thoroughly. Melt the butter in a frying pan and quickly stir-fry the courgette for about 30 seconds. Add the rice, season with salt and pepper to taste and mix well. Spoon into ramekin dishes and press down lightly with the back of a spoon. Unmould onto warmed plates, garnish with parsley and serve at once.

Note: Packets of ready-mixed basmati and wild rice are readily available from large supermarkets.

JULIENNE OF VEGETABLES

175 g (6 oz) carrot, peeled
175 g (6 oz) leek, trimmed
juice of ½ lemon
salt and freshly ground black pepper
15 g (½ oz) butter

Cut the vegetables into fine strips, about 4 cm (1½ inches) long. Rinse the vegetable julienne. Add the lemon juice, salt and pepper to a saucepan of water and bring to the boil. Add the carrot and cook for 3-4 minutes. Add the leek and cook for a further 1 minute or until the vegetables are tender but retain their bite. Drain thoroughly. Melt the butter in a pan, reduce the heat and add the vegetables. Toss to coat in the melted butter, season with salt and pepper to taste, then serve.

RASPBERRY AND ALMOND STACKS

6 sheets of filo pastry
50 g (2 oz) butter, melted
50 g (2 oz) caster sugar
50 g (2 oz) ground almonds
25 g (1 oz) flaked almonds

Crème Pâtissière:

25 g (1 oz) caster sugar
1 egg (size 1), plus 1 egg yolk
20 g (¾ oz) plain flour
200 ml (7 fl oz) full-cream milk
3.75 ml (¾ tsp) vanilla essence
150 ml (¼ pint) double cream
15 ml (1 tbsp) caster sugar

Raspberry Sauce:

225 g (8 oz) raspberries (fresh or frozen and
   defrosted
2-3 drops of lemon juice
5 ml (1 tsp) icing sugar, sifted

To Serve:

225 g (8 oz) fresh raspberries
icing sugar, for dusting
a little single cream
mint leaves, to decorate

First prepare the crème pâtissière. In a bowl, whisk together the sugar and egg, plus extra yolk, using an electric whisk, until thick and creamy. Sift in the flour and whisk until smooth. Heat the milk in a saucepan to boiling point, then whisk into the egg mixture. Return to the heat and stir continuously with a hand whisk until the mixture bubbles. Immediately remove from the heat. Add the vanilla essence. Cover the surface closely with damp greaseproof paper to prevent a skin forming and allow to cool, then chill. In a separate bowl, lightly whisk the cream; cover and chill.

Meanwhile, cut 12 circles of filo pastry, using a 6 cm (2½ inch) fluted cutter and place on a large greased baking sheet. (Keep any pastry which is not being used wrapped to prevent drying.) Using a pastry brush, brush the circles of pastry carefully with melted butter. Sprinkle each circle with a little caster sugar and ground almonds. Cover with another layer of pastry, sugar and almonds. Top with a final circle of pastry and brush lightly with butter. Lay flaked almonds on top of four of the pastries (these will form the top layer of stacks). Bake in a preheated oven at 190°C (375°F) mark 5 for 10-12 minutes or until crisp and golden. Transfer to a wire rack to cool.

To make the raspberry sauce, purée the raspberries in a blender or food processor, then pass through a fine nylon sieve to remove the pips. Stir in the lemon juice and icing sugar. Cover and chill.

To finish the crème pâtissière, fold the lightly whipped cream and sugar into the custard mixture.

To serve, set aside 16 raspberries for decoration. Halve the remainder and sprinkle with icing sugar.

Place a pastry layer (without flaked almonds) on each dessert plate. Spoon on sufficient crème pâtissière to cover the pastry to the edge. Cover with half of the dusted raspberries. (The filling may run over the edge of the pastry.) Repeat carefully with another layer of pastry, them crème pâtissière and raspberries.

Dust the flaked almond topped pastry circles with icing sugar and position on top. Spoon raspberry sauce around each stack. Dot with cream and feather, using a wooden skewer. Decorate with the reserved raspberries, dusted with icing sugar, and mint leaves. Serve immediately.

Dark Chocolate Horns filled with a White Chocolate Mousse
ROGER HEMMING'S DESSERT (Regional Heat)

Raspberry Surprise
ALISON FIANDER'S DESSERT (Regional Heat)

THE HOME COUNTIES
ALISON FIANDER • SARA DOUGLAS • CHRIS RAND

PANEL OF JUDGES
Michel Roux Jnr • Carol Thatcher • Loyd Grossman

CHRIS RAND'S MENU

STARTER
Ginger and Mustard Salmon
"I approve of that" **Michel Roux Jnr**

MAIN COURSE
*Pan-fried Breast of Pheasant
with a Date and Red Wine Sauce*
"That works rather well" **Carol Thatcher**

Smoked Cheese Lyonnaise Potatoes

Carrot and Green Bean Batons

Minted Mangetouts

DESSERT
Layered Chocolate Mousse
"It's very light. Not rich" **Michel Roux Jnr**

Christopher Rand, from St Albans in Hertfordshire, works in the foreign exchange money markets for an Australian bank. His financial acumen is also put to good use as chairman of the steward-ship committee at St Albans Abbey, responsible for fund-raising. In more relaxing moments, Chris enjoys a round of golf at the Brickenham Golf Club.

Ginger and Mustard Salmon

2 salmon fillets, each about 150 g (5 oz)

Marinade:
5 ml (1 tsp) Dijon mustard
45 ml (3 tbsp) white wine
60 ml (4 tbsp) olive oil
2 pieces of preserved stem ginger in syrup,
*   drained and finely sliced*
15 ml (1 tbsp) chopped dill

To Serve:
mixed salad leaves (eg lamb's lettuce and
*   radicchio)*
lumpfish caviar
dill sprigs, to garnish

Cut the salmon into cubes and place in a shallow dish.

Mix together the ingredients for the marinade in a bowl, then pour over the salmon. (It may be necessary to add a little of the syrup from the stem ginger, to balance the marinade.) Cover and leave to marinate in the refrigerator for 2 hours.

To serve, remove the salmon from the marinade with a slotted spoon, reserving the marinade. Place a mound of salmon on each serving plate and arrange the salad leaves to one side. Place a heaped teaspoonful of caviar on each plate and garnish with dill sprigs. Pour some of the marinade over the salad leaves and serve immediately.

Pan-fried Breast of Pheasant with a Date and Red Wine Sauce

4 pheasant breasts
25 g (1 oz) butter
30 ml (2 tbsp) olive oil
salt and freshly ground black pepper

Date and Red Wine Sauce:
knob of butter
4 shallots, finely chopped
3 cloves garlic, finely chopped
75 ml (5 tbsp) red wine
30 ml (2 tbsp) brandy
6 fresh dates, stoned and roughly chopped
24 peppercorns, crushed
15 ml (1 tbsp) plain flour
600 ml (1 pint) chicken stock (see right)

To Garnish:
4 fresh dates

First make the sauce. Melt the knob of butter in a saucepan, add the shallots and garlic, cover and sweat gently until softened. Add the red wine and reduce until the wine has almost completely evaporated. Add the brandy and reduce again.

Add the chopped dates and crushed peppercorns; cook for 2-3 minutes. Add the flour and mix well, then stir in the chicken stock. Allow to simmer for 10 minutes, then pass through a conical sieve into a clean saucepan, pressing the ingredients through to extract as much flavour as possible. Check the seasoning. Keep warm while cooking the pheasant.

To cook the pheasant breasts, heat the butter and oil in a large frying pan. When sizzling, add the pheasant breasts and fry, turning constantly, for 8-10 minutes or until cooked through. Transfer to a warmed plate, season with salt and pepper and leave to rest in a low oven for a few minutes.

To serve, place the pheasant breasts on warmed serving plates and pour over the sauce. Serve immediately, garnished with dates.

Chicken Stock: Put 1.4 kg (3 lb) chicken wings in a large saucepan and pour on about 1.7 litres (3 pints) water. Bring to the boil and skim. Add 2 carrots, peeled and quartered; 1 stick celery, chopped; 2 leeks, sliced; 2 small onions quartered; salt, pepper and a bouquet garni. Lower the heat, cover and simmer for 2 hours. Strain and use as required.

SMOKED CHEESE LYONNAISE POTATOES

4 large potatoes
4 cloves garlic
125 g (4 oz) smoked cheese
150 ml (¼ pint) double cream
salt and freshly ground black pepper
parsley sprigs, to garnish

Peel and thinly slice the potatoes. Peel and thinly slice the garlic. Slice the smoked cheese.

Butter 4 individual soufflé dishes and arrange a layer of overlapping potato slices in the bottom of each one. Cover with a layer of smoked cheese and garlic, then top with another layer of potatoes. Pour on the cream and season with salt and pepper. Bake in a preheated oven at 180°C (350°F) mark 4 for 45 minutes. Garnish with parsley to serve.

CARROT AND GREEN BEAN BATONS

2 plump carrots, peeled
12 fine green beans

Cut two 2.5 cm (1 inch) thick slices from the wide end of each carrot and then remove the centre cores. Thread 4 beans through each carrot ring. Place in a steamer over a pan of boiling water and steam for 10 minutes until tender.

LAYERED CHOCOLATE MOUSSE

Dark Chocolate Mousse:
50 g (2 oz) plain chocolate, in pieces
knob of butter
finely grated rind and juice of 1 orange
60 ml (4 tbsp) double cream
1 egg (size 2), separated

Light Chocolate Mousse:
75 g (3 oz) white chocolate, in pieces
30 ml (2 tbsp) white rum
150 ml (¼ pint) double cream
2 egg whites (size 2)
50 g (2 oz) caster sugar

To Decorate:
4 kumquats, sliced
grated plain dark chocolate

To make the dark chocolate mousse, put the dark chocolate, butter, orange rind and juice in a bowl over a pan of simmering water until the chocolate is melted. Remove the bowl from the pan and allow to cool slightly.

Whip the cream until thick. In a separate bowl, whisk the egg white until soft peaks form. Lightly beat the egg yolk and fold into the chocolate mixture, followed by the whipped cream. Finally fold in the egg white. Divide the dark chocolate mousse between 4 individual glass serving dishes and place in the freezer for 20 minutes until set.

Meanwhile, make the white chocolate mousse. Put the white chocolate and rum in a bowl over a pan of simmering water until melted. Remove the bowl from the pan and allow to cool slightly. Whip the cream until thick. In a separate bowl whisk the egg whites until soft peaks form, then gradually whisk in the sugar. Fold this meringue into the whipped cream as lightly as possible, then fold this mixture into the melted chocolate.

Remove the dark chocolate mousses from the freezer and top with the white chocolate mousse. Chill in the refrigerator for 2 hours until set. Top with the kumquats and grated chocolate to serve.

——— SCOTLAND & N. IRELAND ———

GERRY GOLDWYRE • LESLIE CAUL • KATHERINE RENDALL

PANEL OF JUDGES

Valentina Harris • Nigel Havers • Loyd Grossman

WINNER

GERRY GOLDWYRE'S MENU

STARTER

Pan-fried Fillet of Shetland Salmon,
served on a bed of Roasted Peppers with
a Basil Butter Sauce

"A wonderful combination...very inventive" **Nigel Havers**

MAIN COURSE

Fillet of Aberdeen Angus Beef,
served with a Claret Sauce

Sautéed Morel Mushrooms

Caramelised Shallots

Potato Rösti

DESSERT

Chilled Lemon Mousse, served with Florentines

"It was like a cloud" **Valentina Harris**

———

Gerry Goldwyre's home is a converted Victorian water tower in Eskbank near Edinburgh. Gerry is an architect and painter, and the tower acts also as both his studio and gallery, with paintings hung at all levels. He is a regular visitor to St Columbus Hospice, where he demonstrates his unusual painting skills to the patients. His leisure pursuits include absailing.

PAN-FRIED FILLET OF SHETLAND SALMON

1 red pepper
1 yellow pepper
olive oil, for brushing
4 pieces salmon fillet, each about 75 g (3 oz)
a little vegetable oil, for cooking
salt and freshly ground white pepper
squeeze of lemon juice
knob of butter

Basil Butter Sauce:
300 ml (½ pint) light vegetable stock
   (see note)
40 g (1½ oz) unsalted butter, diced
7 g (¼ oz) finely chopped basil leaves

To Garnish:
fennel sprigs

Quarter the peppers and remove the core and seeds. Roast in a preheated oven at 230°C (450°F) mark 8 for 10 minutes until softened. Remove from the oven, cover with a tea-towel and leave until cool enough to handle, then peel away the skin. Place in a shallow dish and drizzle with olive oil.

To prepare the basil butter sauce, heat the stock in a saucepan, then whisk in the butter, a piece at a time, until thick and creamy. Taste and adjust the seasoning. Set aside; keep warm.

Dry the salmon fillets with kitchen paper and season with salt and pepper. Sprinkle with a little lemon juice. Heat the frying pan until very hot, then add a small drop of oil. Add the salmon to the pan and cook for 20 seconds or until crisp underneath. Turn and cook for 10 seconds until the other side is crisp. Remove from the heat and add a knob of butter. Place in a preheated oven at 190°C (375°F) mark 5 for 1½ minutes.

Arrange the peppers on warmed serving plates and lay the salmon fillets on top. Stir the basil into the butter sauce, then pour over the fish. Garnish with fennel and serve at once.

Note: For the sauce I use a very light vegetable stock, flavoured with fennel.

FILLET OF ABERDEEN ANGUS BEEF WITH A CLARET SAUCE

For this recipe, I always use prime well-flavoured Aberdeen Angus beef, which has been hung for a minimum of 14 days.

4 Aberdeen Angus fillet steaks
15 g (½ oz) duck fat or lard
knob of butter
salt and freshly ground black pepper

Claret Sauce:
300 ml (½ pint) beef stock (made with shin
   of beef and marrow bone)
150 ml (¼ pint) game stock
50 g (2 oz) unsalted butter
1 clove garlic, chopped
4 shallots, chopped
2 thyme sprigs
150 ml (¼ pint) good red wine (eg Claret)

To Garnish:
snipped chives

First prepare the sauce. Simmer both the beef and game stocks until reduced by half. Melt the butter in a saucepan and add the garlic, shallots and thyme. Cook over a moderate heat until the shallots are golden brown and caramelised. Deglaze the pan with the wine and reduce until almost completely evaporated. Add both stocks and reduce slightly. Remove from the heat and strain the sauce through a fine sieve into a clean pan. Reheat and reduce until the sauce is thick enough to lightly coat the back of a spoon. Check the seasoning and set aside.

To cook the steaks, place a heavy-based (ovenproof) frying pan over a high heat. When it is very hot, add the oil or cooking fat. Lay 2 steaks in the pan, moving them to prevent sticking. Cook for 25-35 seconds each side, or until almost cooked to your liking. Repeat with the other 2 steaks. Remove from the heat, add a knob of butter and season with salt and pepper. Put into a very hot oven at 220°C (425°F) mark 7 for 1 minute, then set aside to rest in a warm place for a few minutes.

To serve, reheat sauce. Lay a rösti on each warmed serving plate and place a steak on top. Pour on the sauce. Arrange the mushrooms and shallots on the plates and serve, garnished with chives.

SAUTÉED MOREL MUSHROOMS

Morels are in season for 3-4 weeks during late spring or early summer. In summer and autumn use fresh chanterelles instead.

12-16 fresh morels
25 g (1 oz) butter
salt and freshly ground black pepper
squeeze of lemon juice

Place a heavy-based frying pan over a high heat, then add the butter. As soon as it has melted, add the mushrooms with a little salt and lemon juice. Toss the mushrooms in the pan over a moderate heat until they are tender. Remove and drain off the liquid. Check the seasoning. Serve at once.

CARAMELISED SHALLOTS

25 g (1 oz) unsalted butter
12-16 shallots, peeled
10-15 ml (2-3 tsp) demerara sugar, to taste
salt and freshly ground black pepper

Melt the butter in a frying pan, add the shallots and fry gently for about 20 minutes until cooked through, golden brown and beginning to caramelise. Add the demerara sugar and salt and pepper to taste. Sauté briefly until the shallots are evenly coated with the sugar glaze. Serve piping hot.

POTATO RÖSTI

4 potatoes
salt and freshly ground black pepper
squeeze of lemon juice
75 g (3 oz) clarified butter

Peel the potatoes and cut into fine strips, using a mandoline if possible. Dry the potatoes in a tea-towel, squeezing to remove excess water. Turn into a bowl, season with salt and pepper, and add a little lemon juice.

Melt the butter in a large heavy-based frying pan. Set four 7.5 cm (3 inch) metal rings in the pan. Divide the potato mixture evenly between the rings, pressing well down. Cook over a moderate heat for about 5 minutes until the underside is crisp and golden brown. Turn and cook the other side until crispy. Drain on kitchen paper, then serve.

Note: The rösti can be prepared in advance, cooled on a wire rack, then reheated in the oven at 190°C (375°F) mark 5 for about 5 minutes.

Clarified Butter: This can be heated to a higher temperature than ordinary butter without burning. To prepare, melt butter in a pan over a low heat, then skim froth from surface. Remove from heat and allow to stand until the sediment settles on the bottom of the pan. Carefully pour the clarified butter into a bowl, leaving the sediment behind.

CHILLED LEMON MOUSSE

1½ sheets of leaf gelatine
3 eggs (size 2), separated
75 g (3 oz) caster sugar
300 ml (½ pint) double cream
finely grated rind and juice of 2 lemons

Candied Zest:
1 lemon
1 lime
50 g (2 oz) caster sugar

Secure a greaseproof paper collar around the outside of each of 4 ramekins, to extend 2 cm (¾ inch) above the rim. Soak the gelatine sheets in cold water to cover for 5 minutes until very soft. Meanwhile whisk the eggs and sugar together in a large bowl until pale and fluffy. In a separate bowl, whip the cream until it forms soft peaks.

Remove the gelatine and squeeze out excess water. Place in a small bowl with 45 ml (3 tbsp) warm water. Stand in a pan of hot water until melted.

Fold the dissolved gelatine into the whisked egg mixture, with the lemon rind and juice, and the whipped cream. Place in the refrigerator until the mixture begins to thicken.

In a spotlessly clean bowl, whisk the egg whites until stiff. Fold into the lemon mixture, using a large metal spoon, until evenly incorporated. Pour into the prepared ramekins and leave in the refrigerator for 1-2 hours until set.

To prepare the candied zest, finely pare the rind from the lemon and lime, using a zester. Cut into fine shreds and blanch in hot water for 6 minutes. Drain and pat dry. Put the sugar and 90 ml (3 fl oz) water in a small pan over a low heat until the sugar is dissolved. Add the lemon and lime zest, bring to the boil and simmer for 2 minutes. Remove from the heat and allow to cool. When

the syrup is cold, remove the zest with a slotted spoon and set aside.

To serve, carefully remove the paper collars from the ramekins. Decorate with the candied zest and serve with florentines.

FLORENTINES

40 g (1½ oz) unsalted butter
40 g (1½ oz) sugar
50 g (2 oz) flaked almonds, lightly crushed
15 g (½ oz) hazelnuts, lightly crushed
25 g (1 oz) dried cherries
50 g (2 oz) dried mixed fruit (eg paw paw,
  pineapple and raisins)
grated rind of 1 large orange
30 ml (2 tbsp) double cream

To Finish:
50 g (2 oz) plain dark chocolate

Melt the butter in a pan. Add the sugar and heat gently until dissolved, then bring to the boil. Remove from the heat and add the nuts, dried fruit and grated orange rind; mix well. Pour in the cream and mix thoroughly.

Spread the mixture evenly on a baking sheet lined with non-stick baking parchment. Bake in a preheated oven at 170°C (325°F) mark 3 for about 10 minutes. Push in the edges and return to the oven. Bake for a further 5 minutes approximately, watching carefully. As soon as the mixture is golden brown, remove from the oven and leave to cool and set.

Melt the chocolate in a bowl over a pan of hot water, then pour on to the cooled florentine, to lightly cover the textured surface. Chill in the refrigerator until set, then cut into triangles to serve.

———SCOTLAND & N. IRELAND———

GERRY GOLDWYRE • LESLIE CAUL • KATHERINE RENDALL

PANEL OF JUDGES

Valentina Harris • Nigel Havers • Loyd Grossman

LESLIE CAUL'S MENU

STARTER

*Isle of Man Queenies marinated in Lime Juice
with Dill, Coriander and Sesame,
served with Warm Wheaten Bread*

MAIN COURSE

*Old Belfast Ham and County Down Cabbage,
served with a Grain Mustard Sauce*

"That was terrific" **Loyd**

Selection of Root Vegetables

DESSERT

*Rich Bread and Butter Pudding,
served with Crème Anglais scented with Toasted Oat Toffee*

"It was sensational" **Nigel Havers**

L eslie Caul lives on the banks of the beautiful Strangford Loch, in Newtonabbey, County Antrim with his wife, Emma, and their dog 'J.C'. Leslie is a lecturer in Education Policy at Stranmillis College in Belfast. He enjoys football and is an avid supporter of Sunderland Football Club.

ISLE OF MAN QUEENIES MARINATED IN LIME JUICE, WITH DILL, CORIANDER AND SESAME

450 g (1 lb) small fresh queen scallops
  (in shells)
juice of 1 lime
60 ml (4 tbsp) extra-virgin olive oil
5 ml (1 tsp) coriander seeds, crushed
5 ml (1 tsp) sesame seeds
salt and freshly ground white pepper

To Garnish:
small dill sprigs
lime wedges

Carefully remove the scallops from their shells, discarding the fringe-like membrane. Rinse thoroughly under cold running water to remove any grit.

Cut the scallops into fine slices and arrange on individual serving plates. Sprinkle evenly with the lime juice, cover and leave to marinate in the refrigerator for 20 minutes, then at room temperature for 20 minutes.

Sprinkle with the olive oil, coriander seeds and sesame seeds. Season with salt and pepper to taste. Garnish with dill and lime wedges and serve with warm wheaten bread (see right).

WHEATEN BREAD

Use ordinary plain flour for this bread, not strong bread flour.

175 g (6 oz) wholewheat flour
75 g (3 oz) plain white flour
10 ml (2 tsp) bicarbonate of soda
2.5 ml (½ tsp) salt
300 ml (½ pint) buttermilk

Put the flours, bicarbonate of soda and salt in a large bowl and stir together. Add the buttermilk and mix the ingredients together carefully using your hand; try to aerate the dough as much as possible.

Place the dough on a lightly floured surface and knead vigorously. Shape into a round and place on a baking sheet. Bake in a preheated oven at 190°C (375°F) mark 5 for 45 minutes. Cool on a wire rack. Eat while still warm.

OLD BELFAST HAM AND COUNTY DOWN CABBAGE

1 ham joint, about 1.4 - 1.8 kg (3-4 lb)
1 large onion
6 cloves
1 bottle of medium white wine
1 bay leaf
6 black peppercorns
200 ml (⅓ pint) ham stock
5-10 ml (1-2 tsp) wholegrain mustard
300 ml (½ pint) double cream
½ small Savoy cabbage, cored and coarsely
*   shredded*

Soak the ham overnight in sufficient cold water to cover. Stud the onion with the cloves. Drain the ham and place in a large cooking pot or heavy-based saucepan. Cover with cold water, bring slowly to the boil and simmer for 20 minutes, skimming frequently, to draw out excess salt. Drain and discard the water. Replace with all but 45 ml (3 tbsp) of the wine and an equal quantity of cold water. Add the onion studded with the cloves, bay leaf and black peppercorns. Bring to the boil, cover and simmer for 1¼-1¾ hours until the ham is tender when pierced with a knife. Drain, reserving 30 ml (2 tbsp) of the cooking liquor.

Wrap the ham in foil and bake in a preheated oven at 190°C (375°F) mark 5 for 45 minutes. Allow to rest for 20 minutes before carving.

Meanwhile, simmer the ham stock until reduced by about half. Add the reserved ham cooking liquor and reduce again. Stir in the reserved wine, mustard and cream. Reduce to the desired consistency.

Cook the cabbage in boiling salted water until tender; drain thoroughly. Carve the ham into slices, adding a little flaked ham to the cabbage. Serve the ham on a bed of cabbage, surrounded by the grainy mustard sauce. Accompany with a selection of root vegetables, such as mashed potato, carrot and parsnip.

Rich Bread and Butter Pudding

This deliciously rich pudding is made with *panettone* the festive Italian yeast bread, enriched with butter and candied fruits.

Pudding:
350 ml (12 fl oz) milk
4 eggs
125 g (4 oz) caster sugar
350 ml (12 fl oz) double cream
½ small panettone
40 g (1½ oz) butter

Oat Toffee:
30 ml (2 tbsp) oats
50 g (2 oz) sugar

Crème Anglais:
300 ml (½ pint) milk
3 egg yolks
75 g (3 oz) caster sugar

To Finish:
a little apricot glaze
redcurrant sprigs

First make the oat toffee. Toast the oats under a preheated grill for a few minutes until golden brown, taking care to ensure that they do not burn. Put the sugar in a heavy-based saucepan with 30 ml (2 tbsp) water and dissolve over a low heat. Increase the heat and cook the syrup to a light caramel. Carefully add the oats, then immediately pour onto a baking sheet lined with non-stick baking parchment. Set aside to cool and harden, then break into pieces.

To make the crème anglais, slowly bring the milk to the boil in a saucepan over a low heat. Meanwhile whisk the egg yolks and sugar together in a bowl until light and foamy. Gradually add the milk, whisking constantly. Return to the pan and cook over a low heat, stirring constantly, until the custard thickens enough to coat the back of the spoon; this will take about 10 minutes. Cover and set aside.

To prepare the puddings, bring the milk to the boil in a saucepan. Meanwhile, whisk the eggs and sugar together in a large bowl until pale and creamy. Whisk in the cream, followed by the hot milk. Cut the panettone into thin slices and butter them. Arrange the panettone slices in individual soufflé dishes, about 10 cm (4 inches) in diameter, and pour in the egg mixture.

Stand the dishes in a bain-marie (or roasting tin) lined with several sheets of newspaper. Pour in sufficient hot water to come halfway up the sides of the dishes. Bake in a preheated oven at 200°C (400°F) mark 6 for 40 minutes.

Brush each pudding with apricot glaze, then carefully remove from the dishes and transfer to individual serving plates. Surround with the crème anglais and stud the sauce with small pieces of oat toffee. Decorate with sprigs of redcurrants and serve.

——SCOTLAND & N. IRELAND——

GERRY GOLDWYRE • LESLIE CAUL • KATHERINE RENDALL

PANEL OF JUDGES

Valentina Harris • Nigel Havers • Loyd Grossman

KATHERINE RENDALL'S MENU

STARTER

*Parcels of Marinated Orkney Goat's Cheese
with Dressed Salad*

MAIN COURSE

*Duck Breast Fillet in a Pastry Lattice
with Grapes and Green Lentils
Carrots, Turnips and Mangetouts*

DESSERT

*Dark Chocolate Cake,
served with a Vanilla Sauce*

"It was delicious" **Nigel Havers**

K atherine Rendall comes from Gifford in East Lothian. Katherine's life is currently almost fully occupied by her three young daughters, Ellie, Sally and Georgia... In her limited spare time, her husband George is teaching her the intricacies of golf. To keep fit and get away from it all, Katherine takes to the local countryside for a much enjoyed run.

PARCELS OF MARINATED ORKNEY GOAT'S CHEESE WITH DRESSED SALAD

225 g (8 oz) goat's cheese (preferably Lairobell)
45 ml (3 tbsp) extra-virgin olive oil
15 ml (1 tbsp) chopped parsley
15 ml (1 tbsp) chopped thyme
30 ml (2 tbsp) chopped chives
½ clove garlic, crushed
freshly ground black pepper
1 yellow pepper
1 red pepper
4-8 large spinach leaves

Salad:
selection of salad leaves (eg frisée, rocket, oakleaf lettuce)
30 ml (2 tbsp) extra-virgin olive oil
10 ml (2 tsp) raspberry vinegar
salt and freshly ground black pepper

Cut the cheese into four slices. Pour the oil into a shallow dish, add the chopped herbs, garlic and black pepper, and mix well. Add the cheese, turning to coat well. Cover and leave to marinate for 2 hours at room temperature, or overnight in the refrigerator.

Halve the peppers and place-cut side down under a preheated high grill for about 10-15 minutes until the skin is blistered and blackened. Cover with a tea-towel and leave until cool enough to handle, then skin, de-seed and slice each pepper half into 6 strips.

Blanch the spinach leaves in boiling water for a few seconds only until pliable. Refresh in cold water, then drain well and dry on a tea-towel. Wrap each piece of cheese in a spinach leaf, brush with a little olive oil and place in an ovenproof dish. Cover with foil, and bake in a preheated oven at 220°C (425°F) mark 7 for 8 minutes.

Meanwhile combine the olive oil, raspberry vinegar, salt and pepper for the salad dressing in a screw-topped jar and shake well to combine. Toss the peppers in a little of the dressing; use the rest to dress the salad leaves. Arrange the salad leaves and peppers on individual plates. Top each with a cheese parcel. Serve at once.

DUCK BREAST IN A PASTRY LATTICE WITH GRAPES AND GREEN LENTILS

To make the pastry lattice you will need a lattice roller. This is a plastic or perspex cylinder with 'blades' set in it available from kitchen shops and mail order cookware suppliers. As you roll the lattice roller over the pastry it cuts slits. When the pastry is lifted from the work-surface, these slits open up to form the lattice.

2 Barbary ducks
45 ml (3 tbsp) olive oil
½ carrot, diced
½ small onion, diced
5 cm (2 inch) white part of leek, diced
½ celery stick, diced
1 thyme sprig
1 glass dry white wine
450 ml (¾ pint) good chicken stock
15 g (½ oz) butter
125 g (4 oz) seedless grapes, peeled

Pastry:
125 g (4 oz) plain flour
pinch of salt
75 g (3 oz) butter, chilled
beaten egg yolk, to glaze

For the Lentils:
50 g (2 oz) green lentils, soaked in cold water for 4 hours
1 thyme sprig
½ carrot, very finely diced
½ celery stick, very finely diced
5 cm (2 inch) piece white part of leek, very finely diced
15 g (½ oz) butter

Remove the breast fillets from the ducks; discard the skin and any excess fat. Set aside.

Chop the duck legs and carcasses and place in a roasting tin containing 30 ml (2 tbsp) of the oil. Roast in a preheated oven at 220°C (425°F) mark 7 for 20 minutes, then add the diced vegetables and thyme and roast for a further 10 minutes. Pour off the fat, then add the wine to the roasting tin and reduce over a moderate heat. Add the chicken stock and simmer, uncovered, for 20 minutes, skimming occasionally to remove any impurities as they rise to the surface. Remove the bones and strain the sauce through a fine sieve. Whisk in the butter and season with salt and pepper to taste.

Season the duck breast fillets with salt and pepper. Heat the remaining 15 ml (1 tbsp) oil in a heavy-based frying pan, add the duck breasts and seal quickly on both sides.

Meanwhile make the pastry. Sift the flour and salt into a bowl. Grate in the butter and mix together with a round-bladed knife, adding a little cold water if necessary to bind the dough. Wrap in cling film and leave to rest in the refrigerator for 20 minutes.

Cut the pastry into 4 equal portions and roll each one out to a rectangle, 3mm (⅛ inch) thick and large enough to wrap around the duck breast fillets. Roll each rectangle with the lattice roller to make 4 pastry lattices. Wrap each duck breast fillet in a pastry lattice and brush with beaten egg yolk. Cover with cling film and leave to rest in the refrigerator for 20 minutes.

Drain the lentils and cook in boiling salted water, with a sprig of thyme added, for 15 minutes. Sweat the finely diced vegetables in the butter until tender. Drain the lentils, add to the vegetables and stir to mix. Season with salt and pepper to taste.

Meanwhile cook the duck breast parcels in a preheated oven at 220°C (425°F) mark 7 for 8 minutes or until golden. Leave to rest on a rack in a warm place for 4 minutes before serving.

Just before serving, add the grapes to the sauce and heat through. Spoon a portion of lentils onto each warmed serving plate. Place a duck breast alongside and pour around some of the sauce. Hand the remaining sauce separately. Serve accompanied by mangetouts, carrots and turnips, tossed in butter.

Note: For an attractive finish 'turn' the accompanying carrots and turnips by shaping them into small ovals before cooking in boiling salted water.

DARK CHOCOLATE CAKE WITH VANILLA SAUCE

*175 g (6 oz) quality plain dark chocolate,
  in pieces*
*30 ml (2 tbsp) strong black coffee
  (cooled until lukewarm)*
150 g (5 oz) butter, cubed
65 g (2½ oz) caster sugar
2 eggs (size 2)
25 g (1 oz) ground almonds

Vanilla Sauce:
300 ml (½ pint) milk
1 vanilla pod, split
3 egg yolks
40 g (1½ oz) caster sugar

To Decorate:
a little melted chocolate

Grease and line a 450 g (1 lb) loaf tin with greaseproof paper.

Melt the chocolate with the coffee in a heavy-based saucepan over a low heat. Add the butter and sugar and stir until the sugar is dissolved.

In a bowl, whisk the eggs and ground almonds together until pale and creamy. Fold in the melted chocolate mixture.

Pour into the prepared loaf tin and place in a bain-marie (or roasting tin containing enough hot water to come halfway up the sides). Bake in a preheated oven at 200°C (400°F) mark 6 for 1 hour.

Meanwhile, make the vanilla sauce. Pour the milk into a saucepan, add the split vanilla pod and slowly bring almost to the boil. Remove from the heat and leave to infuse for 10 minutes. Whisk the egg yolks and sugar together in a bowl until light and foamy. Bring the milk to the boil and gradually pour onto the egg mixture, whisking continuously.

Return to the cleaned pan and cook over a gentle heat, stirring constantly, until the custard thickens enough to coat the back of the spoon; this will take approximately 10 minutes. Remove from the heat and cover the surface closely with dampened greaseproof paper. Allow to cool. Remove the vanilla pod just before serving.

Turn the cake out of the tin onto a wire rack and leave to cool for 15 minutes.

To serve, cut the cake into thick slices, trimming off any crisp edges. Pour a pool of vanilla sauce onto each serving plate and place a slice of warm cake in the middle. Spoon dots of melted chocolate onto the sauce and feather with a wooden skewer. Serve at once.

THE MIDLANDS

ELAINE BATES • NICOLA KIDD • MARY WILDE

PANEL OF JUDGES

David Chambers • Michael Ball • Loyd Grossman

WINNER

ELAINE BATES' MENU

STARTER

*Warm Salad of Puy Lentils and Spring Onions
with a Mustard Dressing*

"The lentils I thought were beautiful" **Michael Ball**

MAIN COURSE

Feuilleté of Fish in a Lemon and Herb Sauce

Casserole of Glazed Vegetables

DESSERT

Cranachan Parfait with Tayberry and Blackberry Sauces

"Plays a game of football on your tongue" **David Chambers**

Elaine Bates lives in a former Gatcomb Park estate house in the charming village of Minchinhampton in Gloucestershire. Elaine is an enthusiastic gardener, and keeps busy throughout the winter in her greenhouse. Her other hobbies include bell-ringing in Cirencester's parish church, and producing elaborate wedding cakes to order.

WARM SALAD OF PUY LENTILS AND SPRING ONIONS WITH A MUSTARD DRESSING

10 ml (2 tsp) black mustard seeds
10 ml (2 tsp) yellow mustard seeds
sea salt and freshly ground black pepper
5 ml (1 tsp) Dijon mustard
15 ml (1 tbsp) balsamic vinegar
150 ml (¼ pint) olive oil, plus 30 ml (2 tbsp)
2 bunches of spring onions
200 g (7 oz) Puy lentils, rinsed
3 slices of white bread
a little olive oil, for brushing

To Serve:
selection of salad leaves (eg rocket, lamb's
    lettuce, oakleaf lettuce)

Roughly crush the black mustard seeds with 5 ml (1 tsp) of the yellow mustard seeds, using a pestle and mortar. Add a pinch of salt, some pepper, the mustard, balsamic vinegar and 150 ml (¼ pint) olive oil. Slice the spring onions into thin rounds, then add to the dressing and stir well.

Add the lentils to a pan of boiling salted water and simmer over a moderate heat for about 15 minutes until just tender. Drain, then rinse well with boiling water. Drain thoroughly. Tip the lentils into a bowl and pour over the dressing.

Brush the slices of bread with olive oil and grill on both sides until golden. Cut each slice into 4 triangles.

To finish, heat the 30 ml (2 tbsp) olive oil in a pan, then add the remaining yellow mustard seeds. Cook over a gentle heat until they just start to pop. Tip in the lentils and their dressing and just warm through. Arrange the salad leaves on individual serving plates and spoon the lentils alongside.

Garnish with the toasted bread triangles. Serve at once.

FEUILLETÉ OF FISH WITH A LEMON AND HERB SAUCE

350 g (12 oz) halibut steak
225 g (8 oz) salmon fillet
350 g (12 oz) fillet of Dover sole
bouquet garni
small piece each of leek, carrot, celery
1 lemon balm sprig
1 glass of white wine (eg Chardonnay)
1 egg, separated
150 ml (¼ pint) double cream, chilled
salt and freshly ground lemon pepper
30 ml (6 tsp) chopped mixed herbs (chives,
    parsley, lemon balm)
125 g (4 oz) prawns
450 g (1 lb) puff pastry (preferably home-
    made)
15 ml (1 tbsp) milk
melted butter, for brushing

Sauce:
150 g (5 oz) unsalted butter, chilled and
    diced
1 shallot, finely chopped
finely pared rind and juice of 1 lemon
150 ml (¼ pint) white wine (eg
    Chardonnay)

First make a fish stock. Remove any skin and bones from the fish and place the trimmings in a pan with the bouquet garni, leek, carrot and celery, and the lemon balm. Add the wine and an equal quantity of water. Bring to the boil, lower the heat and simmer for about 20 minutes. Strain through a fine sieve; set aside.

Put 50 g (2 oz) of the salmon and 125 g (4 oz) of the sole in a blender or food processor and work to a purée. With the machine running, add the egg white through the feeder tube, processing briefly until smooth. Pass the fish mousse through a sieve into a bowl. Gradually beat in the chilled cream, then season and add 10 ml (2 tsp) of the chopped mixed herbs. Cover and chill in the refrigerator.

Cut the rest of the fish into small chunks and place in a bowl along with the prawns and another 10 ml (2 tsp) of the herbs. Season with lemon pepper. Toss lightly to mix, cover and place in the refrigerator.

Roll out three quarters of the pastry to a 2 mm (1/10 inch) thickness and cut out four rounds, about 12 cm (5 inches) in diameter and large enough to fit 4 individual curved pie moulds. Line the moulds with the pastry, allowing it to overhang the rim by about 1 cm (1/2 inch). Beat the egg yolk with 15 ml (1 tbsp) milk to make a glaze. Brush the inside of the pastry with egg glaze, then spread a quarter of the fish mousse around the inside of each pastry case. Reserve a few pieces of the fish for garnish; fill the pastry cases with the rest.

Roll out the remaining pastry and cut out four rounds to cover the tops of the moulds; place in position and brush with egg glaze. Seal the overhanging pastry edges with glaze. Turn the feuilletés out of their moulds onto a baking sheet. Brush the outside with egg glaze and mark shallow spiral cuts with the point of a knife to decorate. Chill for about 30 minutes.

Meanwhile, make the sauce. Melt 25 g (1 oz) of the butter in a pan, add the chopped shallot and cook until softened. Add the lemon rind and half the juice, 150 ml (1/4 pint) of the fish stock and two-thirds of the wine. Boil rapidly until reduced by half, then strain through a fine sieve into a clean saucepan. Return to a low heat and gradually whisk in the remaining butter, a piece at a time. Add the reserved pieces of fish and poach in the sauce for about 1 minute until cooked through. Season with salt and lemon pepper to taste. Add the remaining wine and keep warm.

Cook the feuilletés in a preheated oven at 200°C (400°F) mark 6 for about 15 minutes until the pastry is crisp and golden. Brush with some melted butter.

To serve, place one feuilleté, cut in half and opened out, in the centre of each warmed plate, then pour the sauce around. Sprinkle the sauce with the remaining chopped herbs. Serve at once.

CASSEROLE OF GLAZED VEGETABLES

8 baby red peppers
8 baby courgettes
8 baby leeks
8 small pink shallots
25 g (1 oz) unsalted butter
10 ml (2 tsp) sugar
15 ml (1 tbsp) lemon juice
salt and freshly ground black pepper

Cut the baby peppers in half and remove any seeds. If the courgettes are very tiny leave whole, otherwise cut in half. Cut each leek into 3 or 4 pieces. Blanch the shallots, leeks and courgettes in boiling water for 1 minute. Drain and refresh in cold water. Drain thoroughly and mix with the baby red peppers.

Melt the butter in an ovenproof dish, then add the sugar and stir until dissolved. Add the lemon juice, some pepper, and then the vegetables. Turn them well to coat in the butter mixture. Cover and cook in a preheated oven at 200°C (400°F) mark 6 for 15 minutes, until the vegetables are well glazed, removing the lid for the last 5 minutes. Season with salt and pepper to taste and serve immediately.

CRANACHAN PARFAIT WITH TAYBERRY AND BLACKBERRY SAUCES

125 g (4 oz) granulated sugar
300 ml (½ pint) water
2 egg yolks
45 ml (3 tbsp) honey
juice of ½ lemon
60 ml (4 tbsp) whisky
300 ml (½ pint) double cream
60 ml (4 tbsp) oatmeal, toasted

Sauces:
225 g (8 oz) tayberries (see note)
225 g (8 oz) blackberries

To Decorate:
few blackberries

Put the sugar and water in a small saucepan and heat gently until the sugar is dissolved. Bring to the boil and boil rapidly for 2 minutes. Meanwhile, whisk the egg yolks in a large bowl until light. Gradually pour on half of the boiling syrup, whisking constantly. Keep whisking until the mixture is thick and mousse-like.

Put the honey, lemon juice, whisky and cream in a bowl and whisk together until thick, but not stiff. Set aside 60 ml (4 tbsp). Stir the oatmeal into the rest of the cream mixture, then fold into the mousse-like mixture. Divide between 4 dariole moulds and freeze for about 2 hours until firm.

Put the tayberries in a food processor with half of the remaining syrup and process until smooth. Sieve to remove the seeds. Repeat with the blackberries and remaining syrup.

To serve, place a spoonful of the reserved cream mixture in the centre of each serving plate. Turn the parfaits out and place on top of the cream. Pool the sauces alternately around the edge. Decorate with blackberries and serve immediately.

Note: If tayberries are unavailable, use raspberries or loganberries instead.

THE MIDLANDS

ELAINE BATES • NICOLA KIDD • MARY WILDE

PANEL OF JUDGES

David Chambers • Michael Ball • Loyd Grossman

NICOLA KIDD'S MENU

STARTER

*Salmon marinated in Lapsang Souchong Tea,
served with Corn Pancakes and Horseradish Cream*

MAIN COURSE

Devilled Pork Tenderloin in a Port Sauce
Garlic Roast Baby Potatoes
Seasonal Vegetables

DESSERT

Lemon and Passion Fruit Tart

Nicola Kidd, from Nottingham, is something of a high flier, working as an adviser on special projects such as company acquisitions. She recently guided the purchase and equipping of a fashionable Sloane Street couture shop. In her leisure time, Nicola enjoys a competitive game of tennis. She is also a member of the local wine society and attends regular tasting sessions.

MARINATED SALMON WITH CORN PANCAKES AND HORSERADISH CREAM

You will need to prepare the salmon 2-3 days before serving, to allow sufficient time for marinating.

450 g (1 lb) middle-cut filleted salmon
  (with skin)
22 ml (1½ tbsp) brown sugar
45 ml (3 tbsp) rock salt
22 ml (1½ tbsp) Lapsang Souchong tea (dry)
30 ml (2 tbsp) peppercorns, crushed
2.5 ml (½ tsp) five-spice powder
juice of ½ lemon
15 ml (1 tbsp) dry white wine

Pancakes:
125 g (4 oz) cornmeal, or half cornmeal and
  half buckwheat flour
pinch of salt
2.5 ml (½ tsp) baking powder
1 egg
150 ml (¼ pint) milk
5 ml (1 tsp) olive oil

Horseradish Cream:
150 ml (¼ pint) double cream or crème
  fraîche
30 ml (2 tbsp) grated fresh horseradish
squeeze of lemon juice
sugar, to taste

To Garnish:
star anise

Two or three days in advance, remove any remaining small bones from the salmon with a pair of tweezers. Mix the sugar and rock salt together and spread half of the mixture over the base of a shallow glass dish. Lay one salmon fillet, skin-side down, on the sugar and salt mixture.

Sprinkle the tea over the salmon flesh to cover completely. Mix the crushed peppercorns with the five-spice powder; sprinkle over the fish. Drizzle over the lemon juice and wine.

Lay the remaining piece of salmon on top, skin-side uppermost, and cover with the remaining sugar and salt mixture. Cover with a piece of grease-proof paper, then cling film, and place a heavy weight on top. Leave to marinate in the refrigerator for 2 or 3 days, depending on the size of the fish and the strength of flavour required.

Shortly before serving, rinse the tea and spices off the fish and dry thoroughly with kitchen paper. Slice thinly on the bias using a very sharp knife; do not cut through the skin. Cover and refrigerate.

To prepare the horseradish cream, lightly whip the double cream, if using. Fold the grated horseradish into the cream or crème fraîche, with lemon juice and sugar to taste. Leave in the refrigerator until ready to serve.

To prepare the corn pancakes, combine the dry ingredients in a blender or food processor. Add the egg, milk and olive oil and work to a smooth batter. Transfer to a jug and allow to stand for 20-30 minutes.

Heat a non-stick frying pan and brush lightly with oil. Add a dessertspoonful of the pancake batter and cook until lightly browned underneath, then turn and cook the other side. Transfer to a baking sheet, cover with foil and keep warm in the oven until ready to serve. Repeat with the remaining batter.

Serve 3 or 4 slices of marinated salmon per person, accompanied by the warm pancakes and horseradish cream, and garnished with star anise.

DEVILLED PORK TENDERLOIN IN A PORT SAUCE

14 prunes (preferably Agen), stoned
600 ml (1 pint) port
2 pork tenderloins, each 225-300 g (8-10 oz)
25 g (1 oz) butter
salt and freshly ground black pepper
12 rashers rindless streaky bacon (dry-cure)
30 ml (2 tbsp) olive oil

Sauce:

reserved port (see recipe)
2 shallots, peeled
300 ml (½ pint) reduced homemade chicken stock
15 g (½ oz) unsalted butter, in pieces

Put the prunes in a bowl with the port and leave to soak for 1 hour. Remove the prunes with a slotted spoon, reserving the port.

To prepare the pork, split each tenderloin lengthways with a sharp knife, without cutting all the way through. Open out and put a row of 7 prunes down the middle of each tenderloin. Bring up the sides of the meat to form a sausage and secure temporarily with cocktail sticks; smear with the butter and season with salt and pepper.

Place a line of 6 bacon rashers close together on the work surface. Lay the pork on top of the bacon and bring the rashers over the top of the pork, crossing over if necessary. Repeat with the other piece of pork. Cut 12 pieces of string slightly longer than the bacon rashers and tie the meat at regular intervals to secure the bacon.

Put the olive oil in a roasting tin and heat in a preheated oven at 200°C (400°F) mark 6. Add the pork tenderloins, turning quickly to brown. Bake in the oven for 45 minutes or until cooked through and brown.

Meanwhile, make the sauce. Set aside 45 ml (3 tbsp) of the port. Put the rest in a pan with the shallots and simmer over a low heat until reduced to one third of the original volume. Strain the port through a fine sieve and discard the shallots. Heat the reduced stock and add to the port; if necessary strain the sauce through a fine sieve again to obtain a smooth consistency. Add the reserved port and whisk in the butter.

After cooking, leave the pork to rest in a warm place for 10 minutes, then carve into 1 cm (½ inch) thick slices. Serve with the port sauce, garlic roast potatoes and seasonal vegetables.

GARLIC ROAST BABY POTATOES

450 g (1 lb) baby potatoes (unpeeled)
4 cloves garlic, peeled
60 ml (4 tbsp) olive oil

Put the potatoes and garlic cloves in a roasting tin with the olive oil and turn to ensure they are well coated in the oil. Cook in a preheated oven at 200°C (400°F) mark 6 for 45-60 minutes until golden brown and cooked through. Serve at once.

LEMON AND PASSION FRUIT TART

To make your own vanilla sugar for the filling, immerse a vanilla pod in a jar of caster sugar and leave for about 2 weeks to allow the flavour to be absorbed before using.

Pastry:
200 g (7 oz) plain flour
100 g (3½ oz) icing sugar
100 g (3½ oz) unsalted butter, in pieces
3 egg yolks
finely grated rind of ½ lemon

Filling:
1 egg
40 g (1½ oz) vanilla sugar (see above)
2 passion fruit
75 ml (5 tbsp) double cream
finely grated rind and juice of 1 lemon
25 g (1 oz) ground almonds

Candied Lemon Slices:
1 lemon
50 g (2 oz) caster sugar

To Finish:
icing sugar, for dusting

To make the pastry, mix the flour and icing sugar together in a food processor. Add the butter and work until the mixture resembles fine breadcrumbs. Add the egg yolks and process briefly until the dough starts to hold together and form a ball. Wrap the pastry in cling film and leave to rest in the refrigerator for 25-30 minutes.

Cut the pastry into 4 equal pieces. Roll out each piece separately on a lightly floured surface and use to line a 10 cm (4 inch) individual flan tin (with removable base).

Line the pastry cases with grease-proof paper and baking beans and bake blind in a preheated oven at 180°C (350°F) mark 4 for 10 minutes. Remove the beans and paper and bake for a further 5 minutes.

To prepare the candied lemon slices, put the sugar in a pan with 150 ml (¼ pint) water and dissolve over a low heat. Bring to the boil, then reduce to a simmer. Cut the lemon into thin slices, discarding the end pieces. Add to the sugar syrup and cook gently for 20 minutes until the rind is soft. Drain and allow to dry.

To make the filling, whisk the egg and vanilla sugar together in a bowl until thick and pale. Halve the passion fruit and scoop out the pulp. Add to the whisked mixture with the cream, lemon rind and juice and the ground almonds; mix until smooth.

Divide the filling between the part-baked pastry cases. Return to the oven for a further 15-20 minutes until the pastry is pale golden brown, placing a candied lemon slice on top of each flan 10 minutes before the end of the cooking time. Transfer to a wire rack to cool slightly, then carefully remove from the tins. Serve dusted with icing sugar.

THE MIDLANDS
ELAINE BATES • NICOLA KIDD • MARY WILDE

PANEL OF JUDGES
David Chambers • Michael Ball • Loyd Grossman

MARY WILDE'S MENU

STARTER
Thai-style Seafood Ravioli
"I could go for that" **Michael Ball**

MAIN COURSE
Guinea Fowl with Green Peppercorn Sauce
Shallot Tartlets
Carrot Purée
Broccoli Florets

DESSERT
Cranberry and Orange Charlotte
"The sweet was my kind of pud" David Chambers
"Really gorgeous" **Michael Ball**

Mary Wilde, from Erdington near Birmingham, is a reception class teacher at Walmley First School. In her spare time Mary thoroughly enjoys reading, and has formed a 'women's book club' with her friends. They meet once a month to discuss and analyse a selected title. Mary's other cultural interests include visiting museums and art galleries.

THAI-STYLE SEAFOOD RAVIOLI

Fish Stock:
900 g (2 lb) fish bones and trimmings
1 bay leaf
1 celery stick
1 carrot
2 red chillis, seeded
1 onion
2 kaffir lime leaves
6 peppercorns
3 lemon grass stalks
2.5 cm (1 inch) piece fresh root ginger,
    peeled
2.4 litres (4 pints) water

Ravioli Dough:
150 g (5 oz) strong plain flour
pinch of salt
1 egg (size 3)
15 ml (1 tbsp) water

Ravioli Filling:
175 g (6 oz) cod fillet, skinned
8 large prawns, shelled
8 kiwi mussels, shelled
2 lemon grass stalks
2.5 cm (1 inch) piece fresh root ginger,
    peeled
2 kaffir lime leaves
1-2 red chillis, seeded
15 ml (1 tbsp) Thai fish sauce (nam pla)
15 ml (1 tbsp) olive oil
5 ml (1 tsp) chopped coriander
5 ml (1 tsp) chopped basil
juice and finely grated rind of 1 lime
salt and freshly ground black pepper
20 small basil leaves
50 g (2 oz) butter

To Garnish:
coriander leaves

To make the fish stock, chop all of the vegetables and put into a large saucepan together with all of the other ingredients. Bring to the boil, lower the heat, cover and simmer for 20 minutes. Strain the stock through a muslin-lined sieve into a clean pan. Boil steadily, uncovered, to reduce slightly.

To make the ravioli dough, put the flour and salt into a food processor. Add the egg and water and process until a smooth dough is formed; if the mixture is too dry add a little more water. Turn out onto a floured surface and knead the dough until smooth. Wrap in a polythene bag and leave to rest in the refrigerator for at least 30 minutes.

To prepare the ravioli filling, cut the cod fillet into small cubes; cut the prawns and mussels into small pieces. Finely chop the lemon grass, ginger, lime leaves and chilli(s), then place in a blender or food processor with the fish sauce and process until smooth.

Heat the olive oil in a small frying pan, add the seafood together with the puréed flavouring mixture and fry, stirring, for 3-4 minutes until the cod is cooked. Sprinkle in the chopped herbs and a squeeze of lime juice. Season with salt and pepper to taste. The mixture should not be too wet; if it is, fry for a little longer to drive off excess moisture. Cool.

Cut the ravioli dough into 4 equal pieces; re-wrap all except one piece to prevent drying. Dust the piece lightly with flour and flatten slightly. Starting with the pasta machine set with the rollers widest apart, pass the dough through the machine. Fold the dough into three, rotate and pass through the machine repeatedly, adjusting the setting of the rollers by one notch each time to narrow the gap between the rollers and roll the pasta thinner. Stop when the pasta has gone through the last but one setting and dust lightly with flour. Keep covered while rolling the other pieces of dough.

To shape the ravioli, use a ravioli mould if you have one (see note). Dust lightly with flour and lay a sheet of pasta on the mould. Press down lightly. Spoon a small amount of the filling into each section and top with a small basil leaf. Moisten the edges around each square with lime juice and lay another sheet of pasta on top. Run a rolling pin over the pasta and mould to seal and cut the ravioli. Turn out of the mould and leave to rest on a clean tea-towel for a few minutes before cooking. Repeat the process to make a second batch in the same way.

To cook the ravioli, bring the fish stock to the boil. Cook the ravioli in the stock, a few at a time, for 4-5 minutes until 'al dente', tender but firm to the bite. Drain thoroughly and keep warm while cooking the remainder.

Meanwhile melt the 50 g (2 oz) butter in a small bowl over a saucepan of hot water. Whisk in the remaining lime juice and grated rind to taste.

Serve the ravioli on warmed plates, drizzled with the lime butter and garnished with the coriander leaves.

Note: If you haven't got a ravioli mould, shape the ravioli on a lightly floured work surface. Place spoonfuls of stuffing at 6 cm (2½ inch) intervals on one sheet of dough. Brush the edges of the pasta and between the dough with lime juice. Cover with another sheet of pasta. Use your fingers to press the edges and between the stuffing to seal. Use a pastry wheel to cut the ravioli.

SHALLOT TARTLET

You will need to prepare the tartlet cases ahead, ready to fill with the reserved shallots at the last moment, when the guinea fowl is cooked.

Pastry:
125 g (4 oz) plain flour
pinch of salt
25 g (1 oz) butter, in pieces
25 g (1 oz) white vegetable fat, in pieces

Filling:
reserved shallots (from the guinea fowl
  sauce – see overleaf)

Sift the flour and salt together and place in a food processor with the butter and white vegetable fat. Process briefly until the mixture resembles fine bread-crumbs, add 5 ml (1 tsp) ice-cold water and process for a few seconds until the dough binds together. Wrap in cling film and leave to rest in the refrigerator for 20 minutes.

Roll out the pastry thinly on a lightly floured surface and use to line four 7.5 cm (3 inch) tartlet tins. Prick the bases with a fork, line with greaseproof paper and baking beans, then bake blind in a preheated oven at 200°C (400°F) mark 6 for 10 minutes. Remove the paper and beans and return to the oven for 5 minutes or until the pastry is cooked through.

Meanwhile, slice the warm shallots. Fill the tartlets with the shallots and serve warm, as an accompaniment to the guinea fowl.

GUINEA FOWL WITH GREEN PEPPERCORN SAUCE

25 g (1 oz) butter
30 ml (2 tbsp) olive oil
300 g (10 oz) shallots, peeled
4 guinea fowl breasts
600 ml (1 pint) homemade guinea fowl or
chicken stock
30 ml (2 tbsp) green peppercorns in brine,
drained
60 ml (4 tbsp) brandy
60 ml (4 tbsp) crème fraîche
salt and freshly ground black pepper

Heat the butter and oil in a frying pan. Add the shallots and fry, stirring, until lightly browned.

Add the guinea fowl breasts to the pan and quickly brown on both sides. Add sufficient stock to cover the meat. Cover the pan and simmer until the meat is tender, about 7 minutes. Remove the guinea fowl breasts from the pan, wrap in foil and keep warm. Continue to simmer the shallots until they are very soft, then remove with a slotted spoon and reserve (for the tartlets see page 59).

To make the sauce, boil the stock rapidly to reduce until it is slightly thickened. Add the green peppercorns and brandy and cook until the sauce is reduced slightly again. Stir in the crème fraîche and season with salt and pepper to taste.

To serve, slice the guinea fowl, fan out on warmed serving plates and pour over the sauce. Serve accompanied by the shallot tartlets, carrot purée and broccoli florets.

CRANBERRY AND ORANGE CHARLOTTE

2 oranges
225 g (8 oz) cranberries
125 g (4 oz) sugar, or to taste
6 cardamom pods, seeds only – crushed
1 brioche loaf
125 g (4 oz) unsalted butter, melted

To Serve:
icing sugar, for dusting
a little fromage frais
finely pared orange rind, shredded
    (simmered in sugar syrup, if preferred)

Finely grate the rind from 1 orange, then squeeze the juice. Peel and segment the other orange, discarding all white pith.

Put the cranberries and sugar in a saucepan with 150 ml (¼ pint) water. Add the grated orange rind and crushed cardamom seeds. Heat gently until the sugar is dissolved, then simmer for 10 minutes. Taste for sweetness, adding a little more sugar if necessary. Transfer half of the mixture to a blender or food processor and work until smooth, then press through a sieve into a bowl. Stir in the orange juice to make a coulis; set aside.

Add the orange segments to the other half of the cranberry mixture.

To assemble the charlottes, you will need 4 individual round tins or individual pudding moulds, about 200 ml (7 fl oz) in capacity (see note). Cut thin slices from the brioche loaf. From these, cut 8 circles to fit the base and top of the moulds. Dip 4 brioche circles into the melted butter and fit into the base of the tins. Cut thin strips of brioche to line the sides of the tin, dip in melted butter and position around the insides of the tins. Fill with the cranberry and orange segment mixture. Dip the remaining brioche circles in butter and position on top.

Place on a baking sheet and bake in a preheated oven at 200°C (400°F) mark 6 for 25 minutes or until crisp and well browned. Carefully remove the charlottes from the tins.

Transfer to individual plates and dust with icing sugar. Surround with the cranberry and orange coulis, dot with the fromage frais and feather with a wooden skewer. Decorate with orange rind shreds and serve immediately.

Note: I use cleaned small baked bean tins for these individual charlottes, but you can use any similar sized moulds.

The North West

Andrea Ferrari • Maureen Bowe • Graham Underwood

PANEL OF JUDGES

Ken Hom • Jane Asher • Loyd Grossman

WINNER

Andrea Ferrari's Menu

STARTER

*Twice-baked Soufflé of Goat's Cheese
with Red Onion Marmalade*

"That would make a very good luncheon dish" **Jane Asher**

MAIN COURSE

*Fillet of Sea Bass
with a Basil and Pine Nut Crust*

Deep-fried Seasonal Vegetables

"Light and subtle" **Loyd**

DESSERT

*Brandy Snaps and Mascarpone
with a Coulis of Blackberries*

"The brandy snaps were fantastic" **Jane Asher**

From Poulton-le-Fylde in Lancashire, Andrea Ferrari is a student teacher. She has two daughters, Sophie and Julia, who take up much of her time with their activities. Walking on the lovely beaches near their home with Rosie, the family's boxer dog, is a favourite family pastime. When she gets a moment to herself, Andrea is off to the gym for a work-out.

TWICE-BAKED SOUFFLÉ OF GOAT'S CHEESE WITH RED ONION MARMALADE

Soufflés:
250 ml (8 fl oz) full-cream milk
1 shallot, chopped
few peppercorns
1 bay leaf
25 g (1 oz) butter
25 g (1 oz) self-raising flour
2 eggs, separated
salt and freshly ground black pepper
125 g (4 oz) mature goat's cheese, cubed

Red Onion Marmalade:
150 ml (¼ pint) olive oil
3 red onions, thinly sliced
225 g (8 oz) dark soft brown sugar
300 ml (½ pint) white wine vinegar

To Serve:
curly endive
freshly grated Parmesan cheese, for
  sprinkling

To prepare the soufflés, pour the milk into a saucepan and add the shallot, peppercorns and bay leaf. Slowly bring to the boil, then strain into a bowl, discarding the flavourings.

Melt the butter in a saucepan, stir in the flour and cook, stirring, for 1 minute. Gradually stir in the milk and cook over a low heat, stirring continuously, until thickened and smooth. Allow to bubble for 2 minutes. Transfer the sauce to a large mixing bowl. Allow to cool slightly, then beat in the egg yolks and season with salt and pepper to taste. Add three quarters of the goat's cheese. Whisk the egg whites until stiff, then lightly fold into the cheese mixture, using a large metal spoon.

Divide the mixture between 4 buttered ramekins and place in a bain-marie or roasting tin containing enough hot water to come halfway up the sides of the dishes. Cook in a preheated oven at 180°C (350°F) mark 4 for 10-12 minutes until the soufflés are risen and firm. Remove from the oven and allow to cool until required.

To make the red onion marmalade, heat the olive oil in a pan, add the onions and fry gently until translucent. Add the brown sugar and cook until the mixture begins to caramelise. Deglaze the pan with the wine vinegar and cook for a further 30 minutes.

Turn out the soufflés onto a baking sheet. Top with the remaining goat's cheese and place under a hot grill for about 5 minutes.

Serve the hot soufflés on a bed of endive, topped with a sprinkling of Parmesan and accompanied by the red onion marmalade.

SEA BASS WITH A BASIL AND PINE NUT CRUST

25 g (1 oz) butter
1 shallot, chopped
3 cloves garlic, chopped
4 fillets of sea bass, each 125-150 g (4-5 oz)
1 bouquet garni
600 ml (1 pint) court bouillon (see below)

Basil and Pine Nut Crust:
50 g (2 oz) roasted pine nuts
30 ml (2 tbsp) olive oil
50 g (2 oz) fresh white breadcrumbs
20 basil leaves, finely chopped
sea salt and freshly ground black pepper

Sauce:
small bunch of flat-leaved parsley, finely
  chopped
75 g (3 oz) butter, in pieces
juice of 1 lemon

To Serve:
16 cherry tomatoes, skinned
basil leaves, to garnish

First prepare the basil and pine nut crust. Put the pine nuts and olive oil in a blender or food processor and work to a purée. Combine the breadcrumbs and chopped basil in a bowl, add the pine nut purée and mix thoroughly. Season with salt and pepper to taste.

Melt 25 g (1 oz) butter in a large frying pan, add the shallot and garlic, cover and sweat gently until softened. Place the sea bass fillets on the top and add the bouquet garni and court bouillon. Cover and simmer for about 5 minutes; it should be slightly undercooked at this stage. Transfer the fish to a shallow flameproof dish and spread the pine nut crust evenly on top. Cover the dish and keep warm.

To make the sauce, strain the cooking liquid into a saucepan and reduce by about half, then add the chopped parsley and whisk in the butter, a piece at a time. Add the lemon juice and season with salt and pepper to taste.

Place the fish under a preheated hot grill for a few minutes until the breadcrumbs are golden and the fish is cooked through. Place one fish fillet on each warmed serving plate and pour the sauce around. Garnish with cherry tomatoes and basil leaves. Serve at once.

Court Bouillon: Put 900 ml (1½ pints) water in a large saucepan with 1 carrot, sliced; 1 onion, sliced; 1 bouquet garni; 6 peppercorns; 2.5 ml (½ tsp) salt and 250 ml (8 fl oz) dry white wine. Bring to the boil, lower the heat and simmer gently for 30 minutes. Strain before use.

Parcels of Orkney Goat's Cheese with Dressed Salad
KATHERINE RENDALL'S STARTER (Regional Heat)

Individual Layered Savoury Cabbage with a Herb Juice
CONNIE STEVENS' STARTER (Regional Heat)

BRANDY SNAPS AND MASCARPONE WITH A COULIS OF BLACKBERRIES

Brandy Snaps:
50 g (2 oz) butter
50 g (2 oz) caster sugar
75 g (3 oz) golden syrup
2.5 ml (½ tsp) grated orange rind
50 g (2 oz) plain flour
5 ml (1 tsp) orange juice

Filling:
225 g (8 oz) mascarpone
*30 ml (2 tbsp) Tia Maria, or other coffee
   liqueur*
25 g (1 oz) caster sugar

Blackberry Coulis:
225 g (8 oz) blackberries

To Finish:
15 ml (1 tbsp) single cream
icing sugar, for dusting
4 blackberries
mint sprigs

Draw 20 circles, each 7.5 cm (3 inches) in diameter, on 4 baking sheets lined with non-stick baking parchment.

Melt the butter in a heavy-based saucepan, add the sugar and syrup and heat gently until dissolved. Remove from the heat and stir in the orange rind, flour and orange juice. (The mixture can be kept at this stage until required: up to 4 days in the refrigerator.)

Drop 20 teaspoonfuls of the mixture into the pre-drawn circles and use the back of a wet teaspoon to spread out as thinly as possible. Bake, one sheet at a time, in a preheated oven at 180°C (350°F) mark 4 for 10-12 minutes until golden. Leave on the paper for 30 seconds only, then remove with a palette knife and place on a wire rack to cool. If necessary, trim to neaten, using kitchen scissors.

To make the filling, combine the mascarpone with the liqueur and caster sugar.

Purée the blackberries in a blender or food processor, then pass through a fine nylon sieve.

Assemble the dessert just before serving. Reheat 8 brandy snaps in a low oven for approximately 1 minute to soften. Cut the warmed brandy snaps in half with kitchen scissors and flute by pinching one end together. Sandwich the remaining brandy snaps together in threes with the mascarpone mixture, placing a spoonful of mascarpone mixture on top. Position the fluted biscuits on top of each tiered pile and dust liberally with icing sugar. Serve on individual plates, on a pool of blackberry coulis. Dot a little cream on to the coulis and feather with a wooden skewer. Decorate with blackberries and mint sprigs.

THE NORTH WEST
ANDREA FERRARI • MAUREEN BOWE • GRAHAM UNDERWOOD

PANEL OF JUDGES
Ken Hom • Jane Asher • Loyd Grossman

MAUREEN BOWE'S MENU

STARTER
Plaice and Smoked Salmon Parcels,
served with a Nasturtium Vinegar Dip

MAIN COURSE
Duck Duo Chinese-style:
Roast Marinated Duck Breast Fillets
Duck Spring Rolls
"Nice combination of taste and texture" **Ken Hom**
"Delicious and savoury and interesting" **Loyd**
'Seaweed'
Carrot Ribbons

DESSERT
Lemon and Blueberry Meringues
"Excellent" **Loyd**

M aureen Bowe comes from Clitheroe in Lancashire. She teaches sewing, and with a little help from her friends, has raised considerable sums for charity with the sale of quilts and toys. Maureen also frequently helps out with her daughter Susan and son-in-law's fish and chip shop business in the nearby town of Blackburn. Maureen is a keen member of the local keep fit club too.

PLAICE AND SMOKED SALMON PARCELS WITH A NASTURTIUM VINEGAR DIP

For the dip, you will need to prepare the nasturtium vinegar about 2 months in advance.

Nasturtium Vinegar Dip:
300 ml (½ pint) white wine vinegar
2 small shallots, roughly chopped
2 whole cloves
1.25 ml (¼ tsp) salt
1.25 ml (¼ tsp) cayenne pepper
1 cm (½ inch) piece dried root ginger,
  roughly chopped
3 star anise
300 ml (½ pint) nasturtium flowers (see
  note

Parcels:
1 lettuce, separated into leaves
4 small thin double plaice fillets
125 g (4 oz) smoked salmon
small bunch of fresh coriander
freshly ground black pepper

To Garnish:
smoked salmon twists
coriander leaves

To prepare the nasturtium vinegar, put the vinegar in a saucepan and add all the remaining ingredients, except the nasturtium flowers. Bring to the boil, lower the heat and simmer for 10 minutes, then pour over the flowers. Cover closely and stand in a cool, dark place for 2 months. Strain and pour into a sterilised bottle.

Blanch the lettuce leaves in boiling water for 30 seconds. Drain and refresh in cold water. Dry on kitchen paper.

Skin the plaice, then cut each fillet in two, along the centre line. Place a strip of smoked salmon on each piece of plaice and top with a few coriander leaves and a grind of black pepper. Roll up each one, like a Swiss roll, then wrap in lettuce leaves, to make a parcel.

Place the fish parcels in a steamer and steam for 5 minutes; drain well. Transfer to warmed serving plates and garnish with smoked salmon twists and coriander leaves. Serve accompanied by the nasturtium vinegar dip.

Note: Measure the nasturtium flowers in a measuring jug, packing well down.

CHINESE-STYLE ROAST MARINATED DUCK BREAST FILLETS

4 duck breast fillets
15 ml (1 tbsp) honey
15 ml (1 tbsp) dark soy sauce
5 ml (1 tsp) Chinese five-spice powder
30 ml (2 tbsp) rice wine
300 ml (½ pint) stock
10 ml (2 tsp) arrowroot

To Garnish:
spring onion tassels (see note)

Score through the skin and fat of the duck breasts and place them in a shallow dish. Mix together the honey, soy sauce, five-spice powder and 15 ml (1 tbsp) rice wine for the marinade, then pour over the duck. Cover and leave to marinate in the refrigerator for at least 1 hour.

Remove the duck breasts from the marinade, reserving the marinade for the sauce. Place the duck breasts, fat-side up, on a rack over a roasting tin and cook in a preheated oven at 240°C (475°F) mark 9 for 10 minutes. Lower the temperature to 200°C (400°F) mark 6 and cook for a further 15-20 minutes. Cover and leave to rest in a warm place for 10 minutes, while making the sauce.

For the sauce, put the reserved marinade, stock and remaining rice wine in a pan and simmer to reduce by about one third. Mix the arrowroot with a little cold water, stir into the sauce and cook, stirring, until thickened.

To serve, carve the duck breasts into thick slices, arrange on warmed plates and pour on the sauce. Garnish with onion tassels and serve with the spring rolls, 'seaweed' and carrot ribbons.

Note: To make spring onion tassels, trim the onions, then feather the leafy ends with a sharp knife. Immerse in a bowl of iced water until they curl and open out. Drain well.

DUCK SPRING ROLLS

2 duck legs
15 g (½ oz) butter
15 ml (1 tbsp) sesame oil
3 star anise
4 cloves garlic, crushed
10 ml (2 tsp) grated fresh root ginger
1 bunch of spring onions, chopped
2 duck livers, chopped
5 ml (1 tsp) Chinese five-spice powder
15 ml (1 tbsp) dark soy sauce
15 ml (1 tbsp) rice wine
10 ml (2 tsp) arrowroot
4 sheets of filo pastry
melted butter, for brushing

Remove the meat from the duck legs and chop. Heat the butter and sesame oil in a wok, add the star anise and fry for 2-3 seconds. Add the chopped duck meat, garlic, ginger and spring onions and stir-fry for 5 minutes; discard the star anise. Add the duck livers and cook, stirring, for 2 minutes. Meanwhile mix the five-spice powder, soy sauce, rice wine and arrowroot together in a small bowl. Pour into the wok and cook, stirring, until thickened. Turn into a bowl and leave to cool.

Halve each filo sheet to make 2 squares and brush with melted butter. Spoon a quarter of the filling along one side of each filo square. Roll up, tucking in the sides and enclosing the filling to make spring rolls. Brush with melted butter and place on a baking sheet. Cook in a preheated oven at 200°C (400°F) mark 6 for approximately 30 minutes until crisp and golden brown. Serve with the duck breasts.

'SEAWEED'

4 large spring cabbage leaves
oil for deep-frying

Cut out the centre ribs from the cabbage leaves, wash and dry well. Roll up and cut into very fine strips. Heat the oil in a wok and deep-fry the cabbage for 2-3 seconds only, until crisp. Drain thoroughly on absorbent kitchen paper. Serve at once.

LEMON AND BLUEBERRY MERINGUES

Meringues:
2 egg whites (size 1)
pinch of salt
125 g (4 oz) caster sugar
5 ml (1 tsp) cornflour
2.5 ml (½ tsp) white wine vinegar

Lemon Sauce:
2 egg yolks (size 1)
juice and finely grated rind of 2 lemons
30 ml (2 tbsp) caster sugar
50 g (2 oz) butter, in pieces

To Finish:
150 ml (¼ pint) double cream
225 g (8 oz) blueberries
4 lemon balm sprigs
caramel pieces (optional - see note)

For the meringues, line a baking sheet with non-stick baking parchment. In a large bowl, whisk the egg whites with the salt until stiff. Gradually whisk in the sugar, a tablespoonful at a time, adding the cornflour and vinegar with the last spoonful. The meringue should be stiff and shiny.

Spoon the meringue into 4 rounds, about 7.5 cm (3 inches) in diameter, on the lined baking sheet. Hollow the centres, using the back of a spoon. Cook in a preheated oven at 110°C (225°F) mark ½ for 60-70 minutes until pale biscuit-coloured and crisp on the outside. Transfer to a wire rack to cool.

To make the lemon sauce, put the egg yolks, lemon rind and juice, and sugar in a heatproof bowl and beat thoroughly. Gradually add the butter, beating well, then place the bowl over a pan of simmering water and stir until thickened; do not allow to boil. Cool.

Assemble the dessert up to 1 hour before serving. Place a spoonful of lemon sauce in each meringue hollow. Whip the cream until it will just hold its shape, then beat in the rest of the lemon sauce. Gently fold in the blueberries, reserving 12 for decoration. Pile the blueberry cream on top of the meringues. Chill in the refrigerator until required. Decorate each plate with 3 blueberries, a sprig of lemon balm and a few caramel pieces, if desired.

Note: To make the caramel pieces, put 50 g (2 oz) sugar in a heavy-based pan with 15 ml (1 tbsp) water and dissolve over a low heat. Bring to the boil and boil steadily to a golden caramel. Pour onto a baking sheet lined with greaseproof paper and leave to set. Just before serving, break the caramel into pieces.

REGIONAL HEATS
THE NORTH WEST

ANDREA FERRARI • MAUREEN BOWE • GRAHAM UNDERWOOD

PANEL OF JUDGES

Ken Hom • Jane Asher • Loyd Grossman

GRAHAM UNDERWOOD'S MENU

STARTER

*Fresh Tagliatelle
with Smoked Rainbow Trout and Cucumber
in a Smokey Sauce*

MAIN COURSE

*Pan-fried Breast of Gressingham Duck,
with a Jasmine-scented Sauce*

"A distinctive and delicious taste" **Loyd**

Parmesan Parsnips

Saffron Potatoes

Seasonal Vegetables

DESSERT

*Profiteroles filled with Vanilla Ice Cream,
served with a Raspberry Sauce*

Graham Underwood from Lowton in Cheshire is a Personnel Manager at a nearby mill where tyre linings and electric blankets are now produced. In younger days Graham was a keen hockey player and National League referee; he now contents himself with coaching and keeping local youth matches in check. His young daughter, Holly, takes up most of Graham's remaining free time.

FRESH TAGLIATELLE WITH SMOKED RAINBOW TROUT AND CUCUMBER IN A SMOKEY SAUCE

Pasta Dough:
225 g (8 oz) strong plain flour
pinch of salt
3 eggs (size 3)
1-2 drops of olive oil

Sauce:
¼ small cucumber
450 g (1 lb) smoked rainbow trout fillet
50 g (1¾ oz) can anchovies in olive oil
knob of butter
500 ml (16 fl oz) double cream (approximately)
15 ml (1 tbsp) tomato purée
30 ml (2 tbsp) chopped dill
freshly ground black pepper

To Garnish:
dill sprigs

To make the pasta dough, put the flour, salt, eggs and olive oil into a food processor and blend for about 30 seconds until the dough forms a neat ball. Wrap in cling film and leave to rest in the refrigerator for 30 minutes.

Divide the dough into 4 pieces and re-wrap all but one. Flatten this portion of dough and pass it through the pasta machine, adjusted to the widest setting, dusting lightly with flour to prevent sticking. Pass the dough repeatedly through the rollers, folding the sheet each time and gradually narrowing the gap between the rollers until the pasta is very thin. Fit the tagliatelle attachment and pass the pasta sheet through the machine to cut ribbons. Repeat with the remaining dough. Leave to dry for 5-10 minutes on a clean tea-towel before cooking.

To make the sauce, peel and dice the cucumber. Cut the trout fillet into ribbons. Drain the oil from the anchovy can into a frying pan. Place over a moderate heat, add three quarters of anchovy fillets and fry for a few seconds. Add a knob of butter. When it has melted, add the cucumber and fry, stirring, for about 30 seconds.

Add two thirds of the cream and allow to bubble slowly. Stir in the tomato purée. Add the chopped dill and keep warm.

Cook the tagliatelle in a large pan of boiling salted water for about 2 minutes until 'al dente', cooked but firm to the bite.

Meanwhile, add the trout ribbons to the sauce and warm through. Adjust the consistency of the sauce by adding more cream as desired, and check the seasoning. Drain the tagliatelle thoroughly and toss with the sauce. Serve at once, garnished with dill.

Note: If you do not have a pasta machine, roll out the dough as thinly as possible on a clean dry work surface, lifting and rotating the dough frequently. Using a sharp knife, cut into 8 mm (⅓ inch) wide ribbons.

PAN-FRIED BREAST OF GRESSINGHAM DUCK WITH A JASMINE-SCENTED SAUCE

The idea for this jasmine-scented sauce was derived from one of Raymond Blanc's recipes.

2 Gressingham ducks
15 g (½ oz) unsalted butter
15 g (½ oz) caster sugar
150 ml (¼ pint) orange juice
5 ml (1 tsp) soy sauce
120 ml (4 fl oz) cherry brandy
juice of ¼ lime
salt and freshly ground black pepper
1 jasmine tea bag
15 ml (1 tbsp) clarified butter

Remove the breasts from the ducks, discard the skin, then set aside.

Chop the duck carcasses and place in a roasting tin. Roast in a preheated oven at 230°C (450°F) mark 8 for about 20 minutes until well browned. Transfer to a large pan and add water to cover. Bring to the boil, then lower the heat and simmer for about 30 minutes. Pass through a sieve into a clean pan, then reduce over a moderate heat to 200 ml (7 fl oz). Skim off any fat from the surface.

Melt the butter in a separate pan, add the sugar and dissolve over a low heat. Increase the heat and cook until caramelised. Add the orange juice and soy sauce and reduce by about half.

Pour the cherry brandy into another pan and reduce over a moderate heat by two thirds. Add to the orange sauce with the duck stock and reduce to the desired consistency. Add the lime juice and check the seasoning.

Heat the clarified butter in a heavy-based frying pan and fry the duck breasts, skinned-side down, for 5 minutes. Turn and cook the other side for about 3 minutes until browned. Cover and leave to rest in a warm place for a few minutes. Immerse the tea bag in the sauce for a few seconds just before serving.

Carve the duck breasts into thin slices and arrange on warmed serving plates. Serve with the parmesan parsnips, saffron potatoes and seasonal vegetables, such as leeks, carrots and fine green beans.

Note: For saffron potatoes, cook potatoes in chicken stock flavoured with saffron until tender; drain well.

PARMESAN PARSNIPS

450 g (1 lb) parsnips
salt
plain flour, for coating
freshly grated Parmesan cheese, for coating
30 ml (2 tbsp) olive oil
25 g (1 oz) butter

Halve the parsnips and remove the woody cores. Blanch in boiling salted water for 1 minute; drain thoroughly. Combine equal quantities of flour and Parmesan cheese. Toss the parsnips in the flour and cheese mixture to coat evenly. Heat the olive oil and butter in a roasting tin, add the parsnips and roast in a preheated oven at 200°C (400°F) mark 6 for about 40 minutes, turning halfway through cooking. Serve at once.

PROFITEROLES WITH VANILLA ICE CREAM AND A RASPBERRY SAUCE

Ice Cream:
600 ml (1 pint) double cream
½ vanilla pod, split
6 egg yolks
200 g (7 oz) caster sugar

Choux Pastry:
50 g (2 oz) butter
150 ml (¼ pint) water
65 g (2½ oz) strong plain flour, sifted
2 eggs, beaten

Raspberry Sauce:
450 g (1 lb) raspberries
juice of ¼ lemon
125 g (4 oz) icing sugar

To Decorate:
icing sugar, for dusting
mint sprigs

To make the ice cream, pour the cream into a saucepan. Scrape the seeds from the vanilla pod into the cream and slowly bring just to the boil. Meanwhile in a bowl, beat the egg yolks and sugar together until well blended, then slowly add the cream, stirring constantly. Return the custard to the pan and place over a very low heat. Stir constantly until the custard thickens just enough to lightly coal the back of the spoon. Do not boil or it will curdle. (If preferred the custard can be cooked in a bain-marie). Pour into a bowl and leave to cool.

Freeze the mixture in an ice-cream maker if you have one. Alternatively turn into a shallow freezerproof container and freeze, whisking every 15 minutes or so to break down the ice crystals and ensure a smooth result.

To make the choux pastry, put the butter and water in a saucepan. Heat gently until melted, then bring to the boil. Remove the pan from the heat and immediately tip in the flour. Beat vigorously with a wooden spoon until the mixture is smooth and leaves the sides of the pan clean. Beat in the eggs, a little at a time, until a smooth glossy paste is formed.

Spoon the mixture into small mounds on dampened baking sheets. Cook in a preheated oven at 200°C (400°F) mark 6 for 20-25 minutes until well risen and golden. Transfer to a wire rack and split each bun to release the steam. Leave to cool.

Set aside a few of the raspberries for decoration. Put the rest in a food processor with the lime juice and icing sugar and work to a purée. Pass through a fine sieve into a bowl to remove the pips.

To serve, fill the profiteroles with ice cream and dust with icing sugar. Arrange on serving plates and pour the raspberry sauce around them. Decorate with the reserved raspberries and mint sprigs.

THE SOUTH EAST

SOPHIE BUCHMANN • ELAINE FORD • SOPHIE MASKEY

PANEL OF JUDGES

Christopher Chown • Sarah Greene • Loyd Grossman

WINNER

SOPHIE BUCHMANN'S MENU

STARTER

*Salad of Griddled Scallops and Celery Leaves
with Sesame Croûtons and a Walnut Dressing*

MAIN COURSE

*Warm Smoked Duck and Shiitake Mushrooms,
with a Beetroot, Plum and Sherry Vinegar Sauce*

Leaves of Pâte Feuilletté

Noisettes of Spinach and Horseradish

Medallions of Rosemary-scented Potatoes Dauphinoise

DESSERT

*Cream of Coconut Ice Cream in a Citrus Tuile
floating in a Ginger, Lime and Butterscotch Sauce*

"The ice cream was pure coconut" **Christopher Chown**

"Perfect" **Sarah Greene**

Sophie Buchmann lives in Uckfield, East Sussex in a regency
mansion with her friends, Keith, Garnet and Edward. They are
in the process of restoring the mansion which was totally derelict until
recently. The restoration is a five-year project taking in both house and
garden. The new kitchen is, of course, a priority for Sophie.

SALAD OF GRILLED SCALLOPS AND CELERY LEAVES WITH SESAME CROUTONS

6 large scallops in shells, cleaned (corals reserved)
150 ml (¼ pint) milk
duck fat for deep-frying
30 celery leaves
salt and freshly ground white pepper

Croûtons:
2 slices day-old white bread
30 ml (2 tbsp) sunflower oil
10 ml (2 tsp) sesame oil
15 ml (1 tbsp) sesame seeds

Salad:
4 handfuls of lamb's lettuce
small handful of rocket leaves
few red chicory leaves (optional)
7.5 ml (½ tbsp) walnut oil
45 ml (3 tbsp) sunflower oil
15 ml (1 tbsp) white wine vinegar

First prepare the croûtons. Cut the bread into 1 cm (½ inch) dice. Mix the sunflower and sesame oils together and brush all over the bread cubes. Sprinkle evenly with the sesame seeds. Bake in a preheated oven at 180°C (350°F) mark 4 for 20-30 minutes until golden and crunchy.

For the salad, wash and thoroughly dry the salad leaves; set aside. For the dressing combine the walnut oil, sunflower oil, wine vinegar and seasoning in a screw-topped jar and shake well to combine.

To prepare the scallops, remove the corals from the scallops and pierce each one with a knife. Poach gently in the milk for 30 seconds, then drain and cut into smaller pieces.

Heat the duck fat in a suitable pan and deep-fry the celery leaves for a few seconds until golden; drain on absorbent paper.

Cut each scallop into thin discs. Preheat a cast-iron griddle or heavy-based pan until very hot, add the scallop discs and cook briefly until seared and golden.

To serve, toss the salad leaves with the dressing and divide between 4 serving plates. Arrange the scallop slices on top and sprinkle with the hot croûtons and scallop corals. Serve at once.

Note: This recipe is illustrated on the front cover.

WARM SMOKED DUCK AND SHIITAKE MUSHROOMS

To prepare this recipe authentically you will need a smoking box. As an alternative you could roast the duck in the oven instead (see note). To cut the pastry leaves, you will need a leaf from a golden maple tree, about 5 cm (2 inches) across.

breasts from 3 wild ducks (carcasses and
*   skin from rest of duck reserved)*
15 ml (1 tbsp) applewood shavings
15 ml (1 tbsp) jasmine-scented tea
salt and freshly ground black pepper

Pastry Leaves:
225 g (8 oz) puff pastry (preferably
*   homemade)*
1 egg, mixed with 1 tablespoon milk

Beetroot Sauce:
2 beetroot
5 ml (1 tsp) olive oil
2 shallots, finely chopped
livers from 2 ducks, chopped
450 ml (¾ pint) good brown chicken or duck
*   stock (made from the reserved carcasses)*
15 ml (1 tbsp) sherry vinegar
15 ml (1 tbsp) plum jam

Mushrooms:
225 g (8 oz) shiitake mushrooms
50 g (2 oz) butter
15 ml (1 tbsp) chopped parsley

Spinach:
675 g (1½ lb) spinach leaves
50 g (2 oz) butter
15 ml (1 tbsp) good horseradish sauce
*   (preferably homemade)*

To make the pastry leaves, roll out the puff pastry on a board to a 5 mm (¼ inch) thickness. Cover and chill in the refrigerator for 30 minutes or until firm. Using the maple leaf as a guide, cut out 4 leaves from the puff pastry and mark veins with a knife. Cover and refrigerate for another 30 minutes.

Brush with a little beaten egg and milk. Bake in a preheated oven at 220°C (425°F) mark 7 for 10-15 minutes until risen and golden. Transfer to a wire rack, then carefully split into two layers.

To make the sauce, cook the beetroot in boiling salted water for 30 minutes until just tender. Drain and allow to cool. Heat the olive oil in a pan and sauté the shallots until just golden, add the chopped livers and sauté for 1 minute. Pour in the stock, bring to the boil and simmer for 5 minutes. Strain through a muslin-lined sieve.

Peel the beetroot and cut into 1 cm (½ inch) cubes. Preheat a heavy-based frying pan, add the beetroot and pour in the sherry vinegar. Allow to sizzle furiously until the liquid has evaporated, then pour in the strained stock. Add the plum jam and season with salt and pepper to taste.

To prepare the crispy duck skin, cut the skin into very small dice and fry in a heavy-based pan without additional fat for 10-20 minutes until golden, draining off and reserving any fat. Sprinkle the crisp skin with salt and drain on absorbent kitchen paper. (Use the duck fat for the starter.)

To prepare the duck breasts, spread the applewood shavings and jasmine tea in the base of the smoking box. Set the duck breasts, skin-side down, on the rack in the box. Cover with the lid and smoke over a low heat for 20 minutes. Remove the smoking box from the heat and leave the duck to rest inside for 10 minutes. The duck should be very pink.

Meanwhile prepare the shiitake mushrooms, slice the mushrooms thinly. Heat the butter in a pan, add the mushrooms and season well. Sauté for 20 minutes until all the liquid has evaporated. Remove from the heat and add the parsley.

Clean the spinach thoroughly and remove the central stalks; dry well. Melt the butter in a pan and add the spinach leaves. Season with salt and pepper, cover and cook over a low heat for 10 minutes until the leaves are just wilted. Take a large leaf, fold it lengthways and roll up to form a rose shape. Make 12 of these and dab a little horseradish on the top of each one.

To serve, carve the duck into thin slices, discarding the skin. Pool the sauce on warmed serving plates. Place a pastry leaf base in the centre of each. Layer up the duck and mushrooms on the leaf and cover with the top leaf. Surround with 3 potato medallions, 3 spinach noisettes and 3 small mounds of crispy duck skin. Serve at once.

Note: If you do not have a smoke box, spread the applewood shavings and jasmine tea in a roasting tin. Position the duck breasts on a rack over the top. Roast in a preheated oven at 180°C (350°F) mark 4 for about 20 minutes. Wrap in foil and leave to rest for 10 minutes.

MEDALLIONS OF ROSEMARY-SCENTED POTATOES DAUPHINOISE

200 ml (7 fl oz) milk
250 ml (8 fl oz) double cream
4 cloves garlic, crushed
2 rosemary sprigs
700 g (1½ lb) large potatoes
7.5 ml (1½ tsp) salt
freshly ground black pepper
freshly grated nutmeg
15 ml (1 tbsp) freshly grated Parmesan cheese

Put the milk, cream, garlic and rosemary in a saucepan over a low heat and slowly bring to the boil. Remove from the heat and leave to infuse for 5 minutes.

Peel and thinly slice the potatoes. Arrange in overlapping layers in a foil-lined baking tray, sprinkling each layer with salt, pepper and nutmeg. Strain the cream mixture over the top and bake in a preheated oven at 180°C (350°F) mark 4 for 1-1¼ hours until the top is golden and the potatoes are soft. Cover with another sheet of foil and press down lightly. Allow to cool, then remove the foil and lift the potatoes out of the tin.

Using a 5 cm (2 inch) oval cutter, cut out 12 medallions and place on a baking sheet. Sprinkle with the gated Parmesan and reheat at 150°C (300°F) mark 2 for 10 minutes.

CREAM OF COCONUT ICE CREAM IN A CITRUS TUILE

Coconut Ice Cream:
½ x 425 g (15 fl oz) can thick coconut milk
30 ml (2 tbsp) coconut milk powder
300 ml (½ pint) double cream
125 g (4 oz) quality white chocolate, in
    pieces
2 egg yolks
5 ml (1 tbsp) Hoppy's coconut liqueur

Citrus Tuiles:
2 egg whites
125 g (4 oz) caster sugar
50 g (2 oz) plain flour
50 g (2 oz) butter, melted
finely grated rind of 1 lime
7.5 ml (1½ tsp) cocoa powder

Ginger and Lime Butterscotch Sauce:
100 g (3½ oz) sugar
75 ml (5 tbsp) of water
juice of ½ lime
250 ml (8 fl oz) cream
15 g (½ oz) fresh root ginger, peeled and
    sliced

To make the ice cream, mix together the coconut milk and coconut milk powder in a saucepan, stirring until smooth. Add the double cream and slowly bring to the boil over a very low heat. Meanwhile melt the chocolate in a heat-proof bowl over a pan of hot water.

Lightly beat the egg yolks in a bowl, pour on the coconut cream, whisking constantly, then return to the pan. Place over a low heat and stir constantly until the mixture thickens; do not allow it to boil. Stir into the melted chocolate, add the liqueur and allow to cool.

Freeze the mixture in an ice-cream maker if you have one. Alternatively turn into a freezerproof container and freeze, beating occasionally during freezing to break down the ice crystals.

To make the citrus tuiles, in a bowl whisk the egg whites until stiff, then gradually whisk in the sugar. Fold in the flour and melted butter and divide the mixture into 2 equal portions. Stir the cocoa powder into one portion, add the grated lime rind to the other.

Spread the lime mixture thinly into four or five 7.5 cm (3 inch) rounds on baking sheets lined with non-stick baking parchment. Put the cocoa mixture into a piping bag fitted with a fine plain nozzle and pipe a whirl around the outside of each tuile. Feather this inwards with a skewer.

Bake, one sheet at a time, in a preheated oven at 180°C (350°F) mark 4 for 5 minutes or until golden. Allow to cool slightly and loosen from the paper with a palette knife. Return to the oven one at a time, for about 30 seconds to soften slightly, then drape over the top of a bottle, patterned side down. Mould to form an upside-down sun hat, then carefully remove. Repeat with the remaining tuiles.

To make the ginger and lime butter-scotch sauce, put the sugar and water in a heavy-based pan and dissolve over a low heat. Increase the heat and cook until a rich caramel colour is achieved. Carefully add the lime juice, cream and ginger. Reheat gently, stirring, until the sauce is smooth, then set aside for 30 minutes to allow the ginger to infuse. Strain before serving.

To serve, pool the ginger and lime sauce on individual plates and float a tuile in the centre. Put two neat scoops of ice cream in each tuile.

Note: I always make an extra tuile to allow for a breakage! Use the leftover cocoa tuile mixture to make some langue de chat biscuits.

THE SOUTH EAST

SOPHIE BUCHMANN • ELAINE FORD • SOPHIE MASKEY

PANEL OF JUDGES

Christopher Chown • Sarah Greene • Loyd Grossman

ELAINE FORD'S MENU

STARTER

Assiette de Poissons
with Baby Salad Leaves in a Chive Vinaigrette

"Lovely clean taste" **Christopher Chown**

MAIN COURSE

Pan-fried Fillet of Wild Rabbit
in a Juniper and Hermitage Sauce

"Exceptionally beautiful" **Loyd**

Caramelised Parsley Shallots

Timbales of Carrot and Parsnip

Seasonal Vegetables

DESSERT

Muscat and Pelargonium Torte
with an Elderflower-scented Cream

"Beautifully delicate" **Sarah Greene**

Originally from Scotland, Elaine Ford now lives in Bentley in Hampshire with her husband, Rob. Elaine is an international training manager for a pharmaceutical company where she is also responsible for Good Clinical Practice methods. A weekly step aerobics class keeps Elaine fit; she has also recently taken up horseriding.

ASSIETTE DE POISSONS

8 small pieces each of turbot, Dover sole
*   and halibut fillet, each about 4 cm*
*   (1½ inches)*
salt and freshly ground black pepper

Fish Stock:
sole bones and trimmings
knob of unsalted butter
2 shallots, chopped
1 leek, chopped
1 stick celery, chopped
1 carrot, chopped
90 ml (3 fl oz) dry white wine
1.2 litres (2 pints) water
1 bay leaf
few parsley sprigs

To Serve:
selection of small salad leaves (eg rocket,
*   frisée, radicchio, lamb's lettuce)*

Chive Vinaigrette:
30 ml (2 tbsp) white wine vinegar
pinch of salt
freshly ground black pepper
90 ml (6 tbsp) light olive oil
2 generous handfuls of finely chopped fresh
*   chives*
pinch of caster sugar, to taste

To make the stock, chop the sole bones roughly and rinse in cold running water. Heat the butter in a large saucepan, add the chopped vegetables, cover and sweat gently for 3 minutes, without colouring. Season with four twists of the pepper mill, add the fish bones and trimmings and sweat for a further 2 minutes. Add the wine and boil for 30 seconds, then add the water and herbs. Boil for 2 minutes, skim, and then simmer gently, uncovered for 20 minutes; strain through a fine sieve.

Meanwhile, make the chive vinaigrette. Place the wine vinegar and seasoning in a blender or food processor. Add the oil and chives and process briefly until amalgamated. Add sugar to taste. Place in the refrigerator until required.

Pour 150 ml (¼ pint) of the fish stock into a frying pan and bring to simmering point. Season the pieces of fish and place in the pan. Cover with a sheet of buttered greaseproof paper and poach gently for 1-2 minutes, depending on the size of the pieces. Turn the fish over and poach for a further 1-2 minutes until just cooked.

To serve, place a bundle of salad leaves in the centre of each serving plate. Arrange the fish around the salad and drizzle with the chive vinaigrette. Serve at once.

PAN-FRIED FILLET OF WILD RABBIT IN A JUNIPER AND HERMITAGE SAUCE

For the sauce, make a well-flavoured stock using rabbit and veal bones if possible.

8 fillets of wild rabbit
15-30 ml (1-2 tbsp) light olive oil, for frying

Marinade:
60 ml (4 tbsp) Hermitage red wine
30 ml (2 tbsp) port
30 ml (2 tbsp) cognac
2 thyme sprigs
2 bay leaves
salt and freshly ground black pepper

Sauce:
600 ml (1 pint) well-flavoured stock
reserved marinade ingredients
12 juniper berries
125 g (4 oz) button mushrooms, chopped
10 ml (2 tsp) rowan jelly
15 g (½ oz) unsalted butter, chilled and
*   diced*
25 g (1 oz) chanterelles

Mix together the ingredients for the marinade in a shallow dish. Add the rabbit fillets and turn to coat with the marinade. Cover and leave in the refrigerator for at least 1½ hours. Remove the rabbit fillets, reserving the marinade.

Pour the stock into a saucepan and add the marinade ingredients, juniper berries, mushrooms and rowan jelly. Bring to the boil, lower the heat and simmer, uncovered, for 20-30 minutes. Strain the sauce into a clean saucepan. Reduce by half, tossing in the chanterelles towards the end of the reduction. Just before serving, whisk in the butter, a piece at a time, and check the seasoning.

To cook the rabbit, heat the oil in a heavy-based frying pan. Add the rabbit fillets and fry, turning constantly, over a high heat for 3-4 minutes. Remove from the pan, wrap in foil and leave to rest in a warm place for 5-10 minutes.

To serve, slice the rabbit fillets at an angle to give long thin slices and arrange in rosettes on warmed serving plates. Spoon the sauce and chanterelles around the rabbit. Garnish with the caramelised parsley shallots. Serve at once, accompanied by the carrot and parsnip timbales and green vegetables, such as steamed asparagus tips and fine green beans.

CARAMELISED PARSLEY SHALLOTS

12 shallots, peeled
40 g (1½ oz) unsalted butter
10 ml (2 tsp) sugar
15 ml (1 tbsp) finely chopped parsley

Blanch the shallots in boiling salted water to cover for 6 minutes, then drain.

Heat the butter with the sugar in a saucepan over a low heat, then add the shallots and mix gently. Cook over a moderate heat for 12-15 minutes, stirring occasionally. Before serving, add the chopped parsley, tossing the shallots to coat evenly.

TIMBALES OF CARROT AND PARSNIP

225 g (8 oz) carrots
225 g (8 oz) parsnips
2 eggs
30 ml (2 tbsp) single cream
salt and freshly ground black pepper
20 ml (4 tsp) finely chopped parsley

Cut the carrots and parsnips into even-sized pieces. Steam separately or cook in boiling salted water until tender, drain thoroughly. Put the cooked carrots in a food processor and work to a purée. Add 1 egg, beaten, and 15 ml (1 tbsp) cream. Process briefly to mix, then season with salt and pepper to taste. Turn into a bowl. Repeat with the parsnips.

Butter 4 dariole moulds liberally and base-line with discs of non-stick baking parchment. Half-fill the moulds with the puréed parsnip mixture, then sprinkle on a layer of chopped parsley. Spoon in the carrot mixture to fill the moulds.

Cover with discs of buttered foil and place in a bain-marie or roasting tin containing enough hot water to come halfway up the sides of the dishes. Bake in a preheated oven at 190°C (375°F) mark 5 for 15 minutes. Unmould onto warmed side plates to serve.

MUSCAT AND PELARGONIUM TORTE

125 g (4 oz) caster sugar
18 lemon-scented geranium leaves
125 g (4 oz) butter, softened
finely grated rind and juice of ½ lemon
2 eggs (size 2), beaten
175 g (6 oz) semolina
25 g (1 oz) plain flour
100 g (3½ oz) ground almonds
pinch of salt
7.5 ml (1½ tsp) baking powder
45 ml (3 tbsp) Muscat wine

Syrup:
150 g (5 oz) caster sugar
150 ml (¼ pint) water
finely grated rind and juice of ½ lemon
6 lemon-scented geranium leaves
75 ml (5 tbsp) Muscat wine

To Serve:
150 ml (¼ pint) double cream
7.5 ml (1½ tsp) elderflower cordial
muscat grapes

Grease and line a 20 cm (8 inch) loose-bottomed round cake tin. Scatter 15 ml (1 tbsp) of the sugar over the base, then arrange 8 geranium leaves around the edge.

Chop the remaining leaves finely and place in a bowl with the butter, remaining sugar and grated lemon rind. Beat thoroughly until smooth, then gradually beat in the eggs. Fold in the semolina, flour, ground almonds, salt and baking powder. Finally, fold in the lemon juice and wine.

Spoon the mixture into the prepared tin and smooth the surface. Bake in a preheated oven at 180°C (350°F) mark 4 for 30 minutes or until well risen and golden brown.

Meanwhile make the syrup. Dissolve the sugar in the water in a heavy-based pan over a low heat. Stir in the lemon rind and geranium leaves; simmer for 5 minutes, then add the lemon juice and wine. Leave to cool, then strain.

As soon as the torte is cooked, remove from the tin and place in a shallow dish with the base uppermost. Pour the syrup evenly over the surface and leave to soak for 30 minutes.

Lightly whip the double cream, then fold in the elderflower cordial. Serve the torte cut into wedges, accompanied by the elderflower cream and grapes.

THE SOUTH EAST

SOPHIE BUCHMANN • ELAINE FORD • SOPHIE MASKEY

PANEL OF JUDGES

Christopher Chown • Sarah Greene • Loyd Grossman

SOPHIE MASKEY'S MENU

STARTER

Salmon Tarts with Herb Butter Sauce

MAIN COURSE

Poached Guinea Fowl in a Quince and Wine Sauce
Spinach in Noisette Butter
Creamed Potato and Celeriac

DESSERT

Glazed Coconut and Almond Puddings
with a Citrus Sauce

"It's a very comforting pudding" **Sarah Greene**

At seventeen Sophie Maskey from Shoreham-by-Sea in Sussex is one of MasterChef's youngest competitors. Sophie left school at the end of last year and is currently working for a major retailer whilst she seeks out a possible career in catering. Sophie is an enthusiastic dinghy sailor. Her other pride and joy is her silver Mini!

SALMON TARTS WITH HERB BUTTER SAUCE

Puff Pastry:
225 g (8 oz) plain flour
pinch of salt
110 g (4 oz) butter, chilled
110 g (4 oz) lard, chilled
squeeze of lemon juice
about 120 ml (4 fl oz) chilled water

Topping:
450 g (1 lb) salmon fillets
25 g (1 oz) butter, melted

Herb Butter Sauce:
25 g (1 oz) butter
3 shallots, finely chopped
150 ml (¼ pint) dry white wine
120 ml (8 tbsp) white wine vinegar
60 ml (2 fl oz) double cream
110 g (4 oz) unsalted butter, chilled and diced
salt and freshly ground black pepper
30 ml (2 tbsp) chopped dill

To Garnish:
dill sprigs

To make the pastry, mix the flour and salt together in a bowl. Cut the butter and lard into 2 cm (¾ inch) cubes. Stir into the flour using a round-bladed knife, without breaking up the pieces. Add the lemon juice and sufficient chilled water to mix to a fairly stiff dough.

Roll out the pastry on a lightly floured surface to an oblong, three times as long as it is wide. Fold the bottom third up, and the top third down over the centre, then turn the pastry so that the folded edges are at the sides. Seal the edges with a rolling pin. Wrap the pastry in greaseproof paper and leave to rest in the refrigerator for 15 minutes.

Repeat the rolling and folding process three more times, turning the dough so that the folded edge is on the left side each time. Wrap and chill in the refrigerator for 30 minutes.

Roll out the pastry thinly and cut out four 12 cm (5 inch) rounds (using a saucer as a guide). Prick with a fork, then place in the freezer for 10 minutes. Transfer to a baking sheet and bake in a preheated oven at 220°C (425°F) mark 7 for 8-10 minutes.

Meanwhile, make the herb butter sauce. Melt the 25 g (1 oz) butter in a saucepan. Add the shallots, cover and sweat until soft. Add the wine and wine vinegar and reduce over moderate heat until only 15 ml (1 tbsp) of the liquid remains. Whisk in the cream. Gradually add the diced butter, whisking all the time on and off the heat. Season with salt and pepper to taste and stir in the chopped dill; keep warm.

Cut the salmon into thin slices. Cover each pastry round with overlapping salmon slices. Brush with melted butter and place under a preheated hot grill for 2-3 minutes. Pool the herb butter sauce on warmed serving plates and place a salmon tart in the centre of each plate. Garnish with dill and serve at once.

POACHED GUINEA FOWL IN A QUINCE AND WINE SAUCE

Use guinea fowl carcasses to make a well-flavoured stock if possible. Alternatively, use a good chicken stock instead.

4 guinea fowl breast fillets, skinned
15 g (½ oz) butter
1 shallot, finely chopped
1 quince, peeled, cored and sliced
30 ml (2 tbsp) Calvados
150 ml (¼ pint) dry white wine
150 ml (¼ pint) guinea fowl stock
2 thyme sprigs
salt and freshly ground black pepper
150 ml (¼ pint) crème fraîche

Melt the butter in a flameproof casserole, add the shallot and quince and sauté gently until softened but not browned. Pour in the Calvados to deglaze, stirring well. Add the wine, stock, thyme and seasoning. Bring to simmering point, then add the guinea fowl breasts, cover and poach for 8 minutes.

Remove the guinea fowl breasts from the casserole, wrap in foil and keep warm.

Discard the thyme sprigs, then transfer the contents of the casserole to a food processor or blender and work until smooth. Pass the sauce through a sieve into a saucepan and boil until reduced by about a quarter. Add the crème fraîche and reduce again by about a quarter.

Check the seasoning. Slice the guinea fowl and arrange on warmed serving plates. Spoon over the sauce and serve at once, with the accompaniments.

SPINACH IN NOISETTE BUTTER

900 g (2 lb) young spinach leaves
50 g (2 oz) butter
salt and freshly ground black pepper
freshly grated nutmeg

Clean the spinach thoroughly and place in a saucepan with just the water clinging to the leaves after washing. Cover and cook for about 5 minutes until wilted. Squeeze out all excess moisture and chop the spinach.

Melt the butter in a pan and allow to cook until nut brown in colour. Add the spinach leaves, toss in the butter and season with salt, pepper and nutmeg to taste. Divide between 4 warmed dariole moulds and press well down. Turn out and serve immediately.

CREAMED POTATO AND CELERIAC

450 g (1 lb) potatoes
1 medium celeriac
25 g (1 oz) butter
a little hot milk
30 ml (2 tbsp) chopped watercress
salt and freshly ground black pepper

Peel the potatoes and celeriac and cut into slices. Add to a saucepan of cold water, bring to the boil and simmer until tender. Drain and dry thoroughly, then mash until smooth. Return to the saucepan and add the butter, milk and watercress. Reheat gently, stirring to mix. Season with salt and pepper to taste and serve immediately.

GLAZED COCONUT AND ALMOND PUDDINGS WITH A CITRUS SAUCE

Puddings:
3 eggs (size 2)
165 g (5½ oz) caster sugar
65 g (2½ oz) butter, melted
75 g (3 oz) flaked almonds
25 g (1 oz) desiccated coconut
finely grated rind of 1 lemon
175 ml (6 fl oz) lemon juice
175 ml (6 fl oz) milk
50 g (2 oz) plain flour

Citrus Sauce:
450 ml (¾ pint) single cream
finely grated rind of 2 lemons
50 g (2 oz) caster sugar

To Decorate:
grapes

Grease and base-line 6 ramekins. Place all the pudding ingredients in a food processor and process for 1 minute until evenly mixed. Divide the mixture evenly between the ramekins and bake in the centre of a preheated oven at 180°C (350°F) mark 4 for 45 minutes.

Place the citrus sauce ingredients in a heavy-based saucepan over a low heat and slowly bring to the boil. Boil steadily for 5 minutes until the sauce has thickened slightly.

To serve, turn out the puddings onto heatproof serving plates. Pour the citrus sauce around them and decorate the tops with grapes. Place under a preheated grill for 2 minutes to glaze. Serve at once.

THE NORTH EAST

PETER ANDERSON • JENNY DOCHERTY • SARAH JOHNS

PANEL OF JUDGES

Anne Willan • Alan Coren • Loyd Grossman

WINNER

PETER ANDERSON'S MENU

STARTER

Mussels with Rouille

MAIN COURSE

Individual Pigeon Pie with Suet Crust Lid

"The pastry was smashing" **Alan Coren**

"A lovely old-fashioned taste" **Loyd**

Braised Carrots

Baked Leeks

Mash Potatoes with Browned Onions

DESSERT

*Oven-steamed Cranberry and Pear Sponge Pudding,
served with Fresh Cream Custard*

"Delicious custard" **Anne Willan**

Peter Anderson from North Shields is a hairdresser, and runs a busy salon in nearby Whitley Bay with his wife, Fiona. He also styles hair for television productions. Living near to the fishing port of Tynemouth, Peter is often up early enough to meet the returning boats, and select his own.

MUSSELS WITH ROUILLE

Allow 6-8 large fresh mussels per person for this starter.

24-32 mussels in shells
600 ml (1 pint) dry white wine
(approximately)
30 ml (2 tbsp) finely chopped shallots

Rouille:
5 cm (2 inch) piece of French loaf
pinch of saffron threads
4 cloves garlic, crushed
1 egg yolk
90 ml (6 tbsp) olive oil
5 ml (1 tsp) paprika
large pinch of cayenne pepper
salt and freshly ground black pepper

To Serve:
selection of salad leaves (eg frisée, oakleaf
lettuce)
herb sprigs (eg coriander, parsley, snipped
chives)
a little extra-virgin olive oil

Soak the mussels in a large bowl of cold salted water with a tablespoonful of flour or oatmeal added for about 2 hours to help rid them of grit. Scrub the shells clean and pull off each beard. Discard any mussels which remain open on being sharply tapped against a hard surface.

Place the mussels in a large pan and pour in enough wine to cover. Add the shallots, cover and bring to the boil. Cook over a high heat for about 5 minutes, just until the shells open. Remove from the heat and discard any mussels which remain closed; drain. Strain and reserve 90 ml (6 tbsp) cooking liquor. Allow the mussels to cool, then cover and chill in the refrigerator.

To make the rouille, cut the bread into small cubes and place in a bowl with the saffron threads. Pour on the reserved mussel cooking liquor and leave to soak for 10 minutes. Meanwhile, put the crushed garlic into a blender or food processor with the egg yolk. With the machine running, add the oil, drop by drop, as if you were making mayonnaise. When the mixture thickens, pour onto the soaked bread and mix well. Season with the paprika, cayenne and salt and pepper to taste.

To serve, toss the leaves and herbs in a little olive oil until glossy, then arrange on individual serving plates. Spoon a small amount of rouille onto the tip of each lower mussel shell. Serve the mussels on the bed of salad leaves.

INDIVIDUAL PIGEON PIES

4 pigeons
45 ml (3 tbsp) olive oil
8 shallots, peeled
1 thick slice smoked bacon (with fat), cut
into strips
4 rounds of black pudding, 1 cm (½ inch)
thick
150 ml (¼ pint) Madeira
300 ml (½ pint) rich game stock
25 g (1 oz) pearl barley
30 ml (2 tbsp) quince or redcurrant jelly

Suet Crust Pastry:
225 g (8 oz) self-raising flour
pinch of salt
125 g (4 oz) vegetable suet
50 g (2 oz) butter, in pieces
a little cold water, to mix
beaten egg, to glaze

Joint the pigeons. Heat the olive oil in a flameproof casserole and fry the pigeon carcasses in the oil until browned; remove. Add the pigeon joints and flash-fry, skin-side down, until browned. Turn and quickly brown the other side, then remove from the casserole.

Add the shallots to the casserole and fry gently for 5 minutes. Add the bacon strips and black pudding, and return the pigeon joints to the casserole, then add the Madeira. Turn up the heat and cook for 5 minutes. Add the game stock, barley and quince or redcurrant jelly. Simmer for 10 minutes, then cover and cook in a preheated oven at 180°C (350°F) mark 4 for 1 hour.

Meanwhile, make the suet crust pastry. Mix the flour, salt and suet together in a bowl, then rub in the butter until the mixture resembles bread-crumbs. Stir in sufficient water to bind the pastry to a pliable dough. Wrap in cling film and chill in the refrigerator for 15 minutes.

Take the pigeon joints out of the casserole and remove the legs. Spoon a small amount of the cooking liquid into each of 4 individual pie tins or dishes and add the boneless pigeon breasts. Top with the bacon, shallots, barley and black pudding. Cover with more cook-ing liquid, then leave to cool slightly.

Unwrap the pastry and knead lightly on a floured board. Allow to rest for a few minutes, then roll out to a 5 mm (¼ inch) thickness and cut out 4 rounds to fit the top of the pies. Cut leaves from the trimmings. Dampen the edges of the pie tins, place the suet crust lids on top, decorate with pastry leaves and brush with beaten egg. Bake in the oven for 20 minutes or until the pastry is crisp and golden brown. Serve at once, with the accompaniments.

Note: Use the browned pigeon carcasses to make a well-flavoured game stock.

BRAISED CARROTS

12 carrots, with leafy tops on
50 g (2 oz) butter, in pieces
25 g (1 oz) brown sugar

Peel the carrots and trim the leafy tops to about 2.5 cm (1 inch). Blanch in boil-ing water for 2 minutes, then drain and refresh in cold water; drain thoroughly.

Transfer the carrots to a buttered ovenproof dish and dot with the butter. Sprinkle evenly with the sugar and bake in a preheated oven at 180°C (350°F) mark 4 for 1 hour.

BAKED LEEKS

12 baby leeks
120 ml (4 fl oz) game stock

Blanch the leeks in boiling water for 2 minutes; drain and refresh in cold water. Drain thoroughly, then place in an ovenproof dish. Pour in the stock and bake, uncovered, in a preheated oven at 180°C (350°F) mark 4 for 1 hour.

MASH POTATOES WITH BROWNED ONIONS

4 large old potatoes
salt
60 ml (2 fl oz) cream
25 g (1 oz) butter
30 ml (2 tbsp) olive oil
1 large onion, finely chopped

Peel and quarter the potatoes, then cook in boiling salted water until tender. Drain well, then mash with the cream and butter.

Heat the olive oil in a pan, add the onion and fry until browned. Toss with the potato and transfer to a warmed buttered serving dish.

OVEN-STEAMED CRANBERRY AND PEAR SPONGE PUDDING

To prepare these individual puddings, you will need individual pudding basins or sponge tins.

225 g (8 oz) cranberries
60 ml (2 fl oz) port
50 g (2 oz) butter
50 g (2 oz) caster sugar
2 eggs, beaten
125 g (4 oz) self-raising flour
2 large pears
juice of ½ lemon

To Serve:
Fresh Cream Custard (see right)

Put the cranberries and port in a heavy-based pan and cook gently over a low heat until softened.

In a bowl, cream the butter and sugar together until light and fluffy. Gradually beat in the eggs, then fold in the flour.

Peel, core and thinly slice the pears and toss in the lemon juice to prevent discolouration. Grease 4 individual pudding basins with butter and line with the pear slices. Add a generous spoonful of the cranberry mixture to each one. Top with the sponge mixture. Cover each basin with a round of non-stick baking parchment. Transfer to a roasting tin and pour sufficient boiling water into the tin to give a 2.5 cm (1 inch) depth. Cover the tin with foil and bake in a preheated oven at 180°C (350°F) mark 4 for 20 minutes.

Remove the pudding basins from the roasting tin and discard the parchment lids. Unmould onto warmed serving plates, gently tapping the tins to loosen the puddings. Surround with the custard and serve at once.

FRESH CREAM CUSTARD

600 ml (1 pint) double cream
6 vanilla pods, split
25 g (1 oz) caster sugar
6 egg yolks

Put the cream and vanilla pods in a double boiler (or heatproof bowl over a pan of simmering water) and heat gently to infuse the cream with the vanilla. Meanwhile, beat the egg yolks and sugar together in a bowl. Pour on the cream, whisking constantly, then return to the heat. Cook very gently, stirring constantly until the custard is thick enough to coat the back of a spoon. Strain the custard through a fine sieve before serving.

THE NORTH EAST

PETER ANDERSON • JENNY DOCHERTY • SARAH JOHNS

PANEL OF JUDGES

Anne Willan • Alan Coren • Loyd Grossman

JENNY DOCHERTY'S MENU

STARTER

*Pan-fried Scallops in a Vermouth Beurre Blanc
with Basil*

MAIN COURSE

*Roast pigeon with a Truffle and Madeira Gravy,
served with a Gougère filled with a Medley of Mushrooms,
and Steamed Spinach*

"I thought the pigeon was really fabulously good" **Loyd**

DESSERT

*Pâte Sablé aux Fruits Rouges,
with a Redcurrant Coulis and a Vanilla Sauce*

A t seventeen Jenny Docherty from Durham is one of the youngest competitors. In 1992, she was the winner of Future Cooks. Jenny is a pupil at Durham School, where she is currently studying for science A-levels. She is also a stalwart of the school's coxed fours, and in the impressive shadow of Durham Cathedral, Jenny spends many an afternoon on the river. Her other hobbies include designing intricate quilts, with her sister Mary.

Pan-fried Scallops in a Vermouth Beurre Blanc with Basil

12 large scallops, cleaned
clarified butter, for frying

Beurre Blanc Sauce:
50 g (2 oz) shallots, finely chopped
45 ml (3 tbsp) white wine
30 ml (2 tbsp) white wine vinegar
30 ml (2 tbsp) dry vermouth
30 ml (2 tbsp) water
200 g (7 oz) unsalted butter, chilled
salt and freshly ground white pepper
lemon juice, to taste

To Garnish:
finely chopped basil

To make the sauce, put the shallots, wine, wine vinegar and vermouth into a small heavy-based pan. Bring to the boil and reduce by boiling to a small amount of concentrated liquid. Add the water and heat gently. Gradually whisk in the butter a little at a time, whisking thoroughly on and off the heat. Season with salt and pepper and add lemon juice to taste. Keep the sauce warm.

Heat a little clarified butter in a heavy-based pan over a high heat until very hot. Add the scallops and fry briskly for about 1 minute, turning once. Transfer to warmed serving plates and sprinkle with chopped basil. Pour the sauce around the scallops and serve.

ROAST PIGEON WITH A GOUGÈRE OF MUSHROOMS AND STEAMED SPINACH

4 large wood pigeons, plucked, drawn and
    trussed
streaky bacon rashers, to cover
4 knobs of lard
salt and freshly ground black pepper

Choux Pastry:
125 g (4 oz) unsalted butter
150 ml (¼ pint) water
125 g (4 oz) plain flour
5 ml (1 tsp) salt
4 eggs
125 g (4 oz) gruyère cheese, grated
beaten egg and milk, to glaze

Steamed Spinach:
450 g (1 lb) spinach leaves, stalks removed
small knob of butter

Medley of Mushrooms:
175-225 g (6-8 oz) mixed mushrooms (eg
    shiitake, oyster etc), coarsely chopped
large knob of butter
chopped basil, for sprinkling

Truffle and Madeira Gravy:
splash of red wine
200 ml (7 fl oz) well-flavoured game stock
splash of Madeira
tiny sliver of fresh or preserved truffle, finely
    chopped

To make the choux pastry for the gougère, put the butter and water in a saucepan. Heat gently until melted, then bring to the boil. Meanwhile, sift the flour and salt together and tip into the saucepan. Beat vigorously over the heat for 1 minute, then remove from the heat and beat for a further 5 minutes. Beat in the eggs, one at a time, to form a smooth glossy paste. Add all but 15 g (½ oz) of the grated cheese and stir until evenly mixed. Cover the choux pastry with a damp cloth until ready to use.

To cook the pigeons, cover them with streaky bacon rashers and put a knob of lard in each cavity. Place the pigeons in a roasting tin and roast in a preheated oven at 200°C (400°F) mark 6 for 25-30 minutes.

Meanwhile, line a baking sheet with non-stick baking parchment. Using a large piping bag fitted with a 2.5 cm (1 inch) nozzle, pipe 4 rings of choux pastry on the baking sheet, each about 7.5 cm (3 inches) in diameter. Sprinkle with the reserved cheese and brush with beaten egg and milk to glaze. Bake in the oven for about 15 minutes, until golden.

While the pigeons and gougère are cooking, steam the spinach, or cook in a tightly covered pan with just the water clinging to the leaves after washing until tender. Drain, toss with the butter and divide between 4 warmed moulds; keep warm. Sauté the mushrooms in the butter until tender; season with salt and pepper; keep warm.

To make the gravy, transfer the pigeons to a warmed dish, cover and keep warm. Deglaze the roasting tin with the red wine. Add the game stock and boil vigorously to reduce to the desired consistency. Add a splash of Madeira and the finely chopped truffle. Season with salt and pepper to taste.

To serve, remove the breasts from the pigeons and slice thinly. Place a gougère ring on each warmed serving plate, fill with the mushrooms and sprinkle with chopped basil. Unmould the spinach onto the plates. Fan the pigeon slices alongside and pour on the gravy. Serve at once.

PÂTE SABLÉ AUX FRUITS ROUGES, WITH A REDCURRANT COULIS AND A VANILLA SAUCE

Pâte Sablé:
pinch of salt
130 g (4½ oz) flour
100 g (3½ oz) unsalted butter, diced
40-50 g (1½ -2 oz) icing sugar
1 egg yolk
1 drop of vanilla essence

Vanilla Sauce:
300 ml (½ pint) milk
½ vanilla pod
2 egg yolks
15 ml (1 tbsp) caster sugar

Redcurrant Coulis:
300 g (10 oz) fresh or frozen redcurrants
juice of 1 lemon
icing sugar, to taste

To Assemble:
300 g (10 oz) mixed red fruit (eg
* strawberries and raspberries)*
icing sugar, for dusting
mint leaves, to decorate

To make the pâte sablé, sift the flour onto a marble slab or chilled board and add the salt. Make a well in the centre. Place the butter in the well and work it until soft. Add the icing sugar and mix with the butter, then stir in the egg yolk. Draw in the flour and mix until the ingredients are amalgamated; handle the pastry as little as possible. Add the vanilla essence and knead in very lightly. Chill in the refrigerator for at least 30 minutes.

Roll out the dough on a very lightly floured surface to a 3 mm (⅛ inch) thickness and cut out 32 rounds, using a 5 cm (2 inch) fluted cutter. Place on a large baking sheet and bake in a preheated oven at 220°C (425°F) mark 7

for 5 minutes, or until golden. Transfer to a wire rack to cool.

To make the vanilla sauce, put the milk and vanilla pod in a heavy-based pan and heat gently to scalding point. Remove from the heat and leave to infuse for 10 minutes. Discard the vanilla pod. Meanwhile, whisk the egg yolks and sugar in a bowl until thick and light. Stir in the hot milk. Return to the pan or place in a double boiler. Heat gently, stirring constantly, until the sauce thickens slightly, to thinly coat the back of the spoon. Allow to cool.

To make the redcurrant coulis, place the redcurrants in a small heavy-based pan with the lemon juice, icing sugar and a splash of water. Bring to the boil and cook gently until slightly reduced. Pass through a nylon sieve into a bowl, to obtain a clear, glossy coulis. Allow to cool.

To assemble, place 4 rounds of pastry on each serving plate and arrange a layer of red fruit on each. Dust the remaining pastry rounds with icing sugar and place on top of the fruit. Pour alternate pools of vanilla sauce and redcurrant coulis onto the serving plates. Place a few dots of redcurrant coulis on the vanilla sauce and feather, using a skewer. Decorate with mint leaves and serve immediately.

THE NORTH EAST

PETER ANDERSON • JENNY DOCHERTY • SARAH JOHNS

PANEL OF JUDGES
Anne Willan • Alan Coren • Loyd Grossman

SARAH JOHNS' MENU

STARTER

*Roulade of Sole, Salmon and Trout
with a Watercress Sauce*

"I thought it was spectacular" **Anne Willan**

MAIN COURSE

*Fillet of Lamb on a Potato and Celeriac Galette
with Orange and Cranberry Sauces*

Leek Spaghetti

DESSERT

Bitter Chocolate Praline Pudding

"A little bit of alright really" **Alan Coren**

Almond Tuiles

Sarah Johns comes from Seaton Ross near York. She is the deputy head of the equine studies unit at Bishop Burton Agricultural College, and must be one of the few teachers to have a real live horse in her classroom! Sarah also enjoys bird-watching, and spends many an hour in one of the hides at the RSPB bird sanctuary at Black Toft Sands. In her spare time, Sarah makes bears and a cottage industry in teddy bear manufacture is developing at her home!

ROULADE OF SOLE, SALMON AND TROUT

50 g (2 oz) smoked salmon pieces
50 g (2 oz) cream cheese
25 g (1 oz) unsalted butter, softened
salt and freshly ground black pepper
2 large fillets lemon sole, skinned
125 g (4 oz) smoked trout slices
2 bunches of watercress, stalks removed
600 ml (1 pint) fish stock
300 ml (½ pint) double cream
 (approximately)

To Garnish:
15 ml (1 tbsp) pink peppercorns in brine,
 drained
few watercress leaves

Put the smoked salmon pieces and cream cheese in a food processor or blender. Add the softened butter and work until smooth. Season with salt and pepper to taste.

Lay the sole, skinned-side up, on a clean surface. Cover each one with a layer of smoked trout, then spread with the smoked salmon pâté and top with a single layer of watercress leaves. Roll up carefully and tie with fine cotton string to secure. Chill thoroughly.

Pour the fish stock into a small saucepan and bring slowly to the boil. Add the fish and poach gently for approximately 10 minutes, then remove. Cover the fish and keep warm.

Boil the stock rapidly to reduce by half, then blend with the rest of the watercress in a food processor or blender. Return to a clean pan and add cream to taste. Adjust the seasoning if necessary.

To serve, cut the roulades into slices, allowing three per person. Pool the watercress sauce on warmed serving plates and arrange the roulade slices on top. Serve at once, garnished with pink peppercorns and watercress leaves.

FILLET OF LAMB ON A POTATO AND CELERIAC GALETTE

2 fillets of lamb (taken from loin)
salt and freshly ground black pepper
25 g (1 oz) unsalted butter
25 ml (1 fl oz) extra-virgin olive oil

Orange Sauce:
25 g (1 oz) unsalted butter
25 g (1 oz) plain flour
juice of 4 oranges
finely grated rind of 1 orange
30 ml (2 tbsp) Cointreau
a little caster sugar, to taste
pinch of salt

Cranberry Sauce:
½ x 190 g (6½ oz) jar cranberry jelly
 (preferably homemade)
150 ml (¼ pint) red wine
15 ml (1 tbsp) balsamic vinegar
 (approximately)
a little caster sugar to taste, (optional)

Galettes:
2 large waxy potatoes
¼ head of celeriac
5 ml (1 tsp) chopped rosemary leaves
25 g (1 oz) clarified butter, melted

To Garnish:
rosemary sprigs

First make the sauces. For the orange sauce, melt the butter in a pan, add the flour and cook, stirring, for 1-2 minutes. Gradually add the orange juice, stirring constantly. Add the orange rind and bring to the boil, stirring all the time. Cook, stirring, for 1-2 minutes, until the sauce is smooth, shiny and of a light coating consistency. Add the Cointreau, then sugar and salt to taste.

To make the cranberry sauce, put the cranberry jelly in a pan over a low heat and heat gently until melted. Meanwhile, put the red wine in another pan and reduce by boiling rapidly to half the original quantity. If the melted cranberry jelly is not completely clear, pass it through a muslin-lined sieve. Mix with the reduced wine. Add the balsamic vinegar to taste and sweeten with a little sugar if necessary. Simmer until the sauce has the same consistency as the orange sauce.

For the galettes, peel the potatoes and celeriac and grate coarsely. Rinse in cold water to remove excess starch, then drain thoroughly and dry on a clean tea-towel. Turn into a bowl, season liberally and mix in the chopped rosemary. Stir in the melted butter.

Preheat a heavy-based frying pan and when hot, tip in the galette mixture. Spread evenly and press down with the back of a spoon. Fry, turning frequently, until well browned and cooked through.

Season the lamb with salt and pepper. Heat the butter and olive oil in a heavy-based frying pan, add the lamb and seal quickly on all sides over a high heat. Lower the heat to moderate and continue to sauté the lamb for approximately 4-5 minutes each side until cooked, but still pink in the middle. Remove from the pan, cover and allow the meat to rest for 10 minutes in a warm place.

To serve, slice the lamb thinly. Using a suitable pastry cutter, cut out 4 rounds from the galette. Spoon two pools of each sauce on opposite sides of each warmed serving plate and place a potato galette in the centre. Arrange the lamb slices around the galette and garnish with rosemary sprigs. Serve at once, accompanied by the leek spaghetti.

LEEK SPAGHETTI

2 leeks, trimmed
50 g (2 oz) unsalted butter
300 ml (½ pint) double cream
freshly ground sea salt and black pepper
freshly grated nutmeg

Finely slice the leeks lengthways into thin 'spaghetti'. Rinse in cold water; drain thoroughly.

Melt the butter in a large saucepan. Add the leeks and cover the pan with a tight-fitting lid or foil. Cook over a low heat for about 10 minutes or until the leeks are soft, but still retain some 'bite'.

Add the cream, salt, pepper and nutmeg to taste. Heat gently and simmer to reduce the sauce slightly, stirring to coat the leeks in the sauce.

To serve, using a fork and spoon, twirl the leek spaghetti to make 'turbans'. Serve each one in a pool of the cream sauce, with a little sauce poured over the top.

BITTER CHOCOLATE PRALINE PUDDING

125 g (4 oz) bitter chocolate, in pieces
50 g (2 oz) caster sugar
50 g (2 oz) shelled almonds (with skins)
15 ml (1 tbsp) brandy
2 eggs (size 2), separated
300 ml (½ pint) double cream, lightly
  whipped

Caramel Shapes:
50 g (2 oz) caster sugar

Carefully melt the chocolate in the top of a double boiler or in a heatproof bowl over a saucepan of hot water.

Put the sugar and almonds in a heavy-based pan over a low heat until the sugar is dissolved. Increase the heat to moderate and cook until the sugar turns to a deep golden brown caramel; turn the almonds individually if necessary to ensure they brown evenly. Immediately turn the mixture onto a lightly oiled baking tray and leave to cool and harden.

Stir the brandy into the melted chocolate, then add the egg yolks, stirring until smooth. Fold in half of the lightly whipped cream.

In a separate bowl, whisk the egg whites until they form soft peaks, then carefully fold into the chocolate mixture. Pour into individual serving glasses and chill in the refrigerator for at least 2 hours.

Meanwhile, make the caramel shapes for the decoration. Put the caster sugar in a heavy-based pan over a low heat until melted. Increase the heat and cook to a golden brown caramel. Using a tablespoon, immediately drizzle shapes onto a tray lined with non-stick baking parchment and leave to cool and set.

When the praline mixture has cooled, break it up roughly and grind to a powder in a food processor or blender.

Just before serving, sprinkle a layer of praline on top of each pudding, then cover with the remaining whipped cream. Decorate with the caramel shapes and serve with almond tuiles.

ALMOND TUILES

30 g (1¼ oz) plain flour
30 g (1¼ oz) icing sugar
1 (size 2) egg white
30 g (1¼ oz) unsalted butter, melted and
  cooled
few drops of almond essence

Line two baking sheets with non-stick baking parchment. Sift the flour and icing sugar together into a bowl. Mix in the egg white, butter and almond essence. Place two teaspoonfuls of the mixture, well apart, on each lined baking sheet and spread thinly to a strip, approximately 15 cm (6 inches) long and 1 cm (½ inch) wide.

Bake, one sheet at a time, in a preheated oven at 220°C (425°F) mark 7 for 3-4 minutes until the edges of each biscuit are golden brown, but the centre is still pale. Immediately the biscuits are removed from the oven, loosen each one with a palette knife and wrap quickly around a wooden spoon handle to form a spiral. Cool on a wire rack.

Repeat this procedure until you have used up all of the mixture; there should be sufficient to make 10-12 tuiles.

Once each biscuit is cool, carefully slide off the wooden spoon handle. Store in an airtight tin if they are not to be served immediately.

Note: You will need to work very quickly once the biscuits are removed from the oven so it is important to bake one sheet at a time.

THE EAST

CONNIE STEVENS • KATINA BEALE • SARAH DYSON

PANEL OF JUDGES

Pat McDonald • Rick Wakeman • Loyd Grossman

WINNER

CONNIE STEVENS' MENU

STARTER

*Individual Layered Savoury Cabbage
with a Herb Juice*

"Adventurous and almost dangerous" **Rick Wakeman**

MAIN COURSE

*Wild Salmon filled with Spinach Mousse
in a Puff Pastry Parcel on a Tomato Butter Sauce*

"I'd pick it every time" **Rick Wakeman**

Timbale of Spinach

Cucumber and Mixed Green Salad

DESSERT

*Pears poached in Pineau des Charentais
with Gingered Butterscotch Sauce and Citrus Crème*

Connie Stevens from Gamlingay in Cambridgeshire works as a marketing consultant in publishing. Last year she was the runner up in Anglia's 'Host of the Year' contest. Connie's leisure pursuits include Formula First racing at Brands Hatch. Back at home Connie is a regular at the local auctions.

INDIVIDUAL LAYERED SAVOURY CABBAGE WITH A HERB JUICE

These quantities are sufficient to serve 8 as a starter, or 4 as a main course. Any unused stuffing can be frozen for future use.

1 Savoy cabbage
2 vegetable stock cubes, crumbled
8 rashers smoked back bacon, or 12 rashers
  streaky bacon
2.5 ml (½ tsp) ground coriander
100 g (3½ oz) butter
salt and freshly ground black pepper

Stuffing:
2 rashers unsmoked back bacon, derinded
1 lamb's kidney, skinned and cored
1 red apple, peeled and cored
2 ripe tomatoes, skinned
40 g (1½ oz) butter, melted
5 shallots, finely chopped
150 g (5 oz) fresh white breadcrumbs
10 ml (2 tsp) very finely chopped parsley
10 ml (2 tsp) very finely chopped thyme
15 ml (1 tbsp) very finely chopped chives
1 egg, beaten
salt and freshly ground black pepper

Herb Juice:
small coriander, tarragon or parsley sprigs

Carefully remove the first six outer leaves of the cabbage. Cut out the hard 'V' core and rinse the leaves. Bring a 5 cm (2 inch) depth of water to the boil in a saucepan. Add the leaves, cover and cook for 2-3 minutes. Drain, reserving the liquid. Pat dry with kitchen paper; set aside.

Separate the remaining cabbage leaves and place in a pan with the reserved cooking liquid, 300 ml (½ pint) boiling water and the stock cubes. Cover and cook for 2 minutes, until just tender. Drain, reserving the liquid. Roughly chop this cabbage and mix with the coriander, 15 g (½ oz) butter and pepper to taste. Set aside.

To make the stuffing, finely chop the bacon and kidney. Finely dice the apple and tomatoes. Heat 15 g (½ oz) of the butter in a pan and sauté the shallots for 2 minutes, without colouring. Add the bacon and kidney and cook for 2 minutes. Add the diced tomato and apple and cook for a further 1 minute. Remove from the heat and add the breadcrumbs, herbs, remaining 25 g (1 oz) melted butter, egg and seasoning.

Brush 4 individual pudding basins or similar moulds with melted butter. Line with muslin, allowing the edges to over-hang the sides. Line each basin with bacon rashers, allowing them to over-hang. Mould 1 outer cabbage leaf around the inside of each basin. Put a layer of stuffing in the middle and press down firmly. Add a layer of chopped, buttered cabbage mixture, pressing down firmly. Repeat the layers until they extend 1 cm (½ inch) above the top, ending with a thin layer of cabbage.

Cover the top with a halved outer cabbage leaf, tucking the ends down the side. Lift up the overhanging bacon rashers and mould them over the top of the cabbage leaf. Pull the edges of the muslin together over the top and tie with string. Bake in a preheated oven at 180°C (350°F) mark 4, for 40 minutes.

Meanwhile, add tiny sprigs of herbs to the retained cooking liquid and leave to infuse until 5 minutes before the cabbages are cooked, then reheat the juice in the pan and strain.

Unmould the cabbages and remove the muslin. Carefully remove the outer bacon rashers; chop some of these to use as a garnish if desired. Place an 'individual cabbage' in the centre of each warmed serving plate and surround with the hot herb juice. Garnish with fresh herb sprigs, and bacon if using.

WILD SALMON FILLED WITH SPINACH MOUSSE IN A PUFF PASTRY PARCEL

4 fillets of wild salmon
1 egg, beaten
450 g (1 lb) ready-prepared puff pastry

Spinach Moulds:
1 kg (2¼ lb) trimmed baby spinach leaves
25 g (1 oz) butter, melted
200 ml (7 fl oz) crème fraîche
salt and freshly ground black pepper
2 egg whites (size 2)

Tomato Butter Sauce:
300 g (10 oz) ripe, full-flavoured tomatoes
40 g (1½ oz) unsalted butter, chilled and diced
5 ml (1 tsp) caster sugar
2.5 ml (½ tsp) cayenne pepper

To Garnish:
diced skinned tomato
8 baby spinach leaves

First prepare the spinach. Cook either in a steamer or in a covered pan with just the water clinging to the leaves after washing for 3 minutes. Refresh in cold water and squeeze dry. Thoroughly pat dry on kitchen paper.

Butter 4 individual moulds. Put the remaining butter in a pan on a high heat, add the spinach and cook for 2-3 minutes; do not allow to brown. Drain off any excess butter, then chop finely or purée in a food processor.

Put the crème fraîche in a small pan and reduce by one third over a medium heat. Add to the chopped spinach and season. In a bowl, whisk the egg whites until soft peaks form, then fold into the spinach. Set aside a small quantity for stuffing the salmon. Spoon the remaining mixture into the prepared moulds and place in a bain-marie, or roasting tin containing enough hot water to come halfway up the sides. Bake in a preheated oven at 180°C (350°F) mark 4 for 15-20 minutes.

Meanwhile make the salmon parcels. Roll out the pastry to a 3-5 mm (⅛-¼ inch) thickness. Cut out 4 rectangles large enough to wrap the salmon fillets in. Cut a slit in the centre of each salmon fillet and insert the reserved spinach mousse; do not overfill.

Place a stuffed salmon fillet on one side of each pastry rectangle. Brush the pastry edges with beaten egg and fold the pastry over the salmon to enclose and form a neat parcel. Press the edges together firmly. Brush the top of the parcel with more beaten egg. Decorate with shapes cut from the pastry trimmings. Brush with beaten egg to glaze. Make two small slits in the top of each parcel. Bake in a preheated oven at 200°C (400°F) mark 6 for 15 minutes or until the pastry is crisp and golden brown.

Meanwhile, make the tomato butter sauce. Halve, skin and deseed a third of the tomatoes. Place in a blender or food processor with the rest of the tomatoes and blend well. Pass the blended tomatoes through a sieve into a small pan, pressing them through with the back of a spoon. Warm gently over a low heat; do not to allow to boil or it will separate. Whisk in the butter, a piece at a time, on and off the heat. Taste and add sugar, salt and cayenne pepper.

To serve, place a salmon parcel on each warmed serving plate. Unmould a spinach mousse onto each plate and add a portion of tomato butter sauce. Garnish with diced tomato and spinach leaves. Serve at once.

POACHED PEARS WITH GINGERED BUTTERSCOTCH SAUCE AND CITRUS CRÈME

4 ruby oranges
1 lemon, halved
6 ripe pears (Comice or William)
150 ml (¼ pint) Pineau des Charentais
200 ml (7 fl oz) dry white wine
125 g (4 oz) caster sugar
1 vanilla pod
10 ml (2 tsp) vanilla essence
175 ml (6 fl oz) ruby orange juice
550 ml (18 fl oz) water (approximately)

Citrus Crème:
120-150 ml (4-5 fl oz) double cream
juice of ½ lemon, or to taste
25 g (1 oz) icing sugar

Gingered Butterscotch Sauce:
60 ml (2 fl oz) water
15 ml (1 tbsp) liquid glucose
100 g (3½ oz) caster sugar
juice of ½ lime, or more to taste
500 ml (16 fl oz) double cream
50 g (2 oz) fresh root ginger, rinsed and roughly chopped

To Decorate:
4 dill or mint sprigs

Cut the oranges and one lemon half into fine slices, discarding the pips, but leaving the peel intact. Peel, halve and core the pears, then rub with the other lemon half to prevent discolouration.

Place the pears in a large pan. Add the Pineau des Charentais, white wine, sugar, vanilla pod and essence. Pour in the ruby orange juice and sufficient water to cover the pears. Add the orange and lemon slices. Bring to the boil and cover the surface with a circle of greaseproof paper which has a hole in the middle. Cook over a medium heat for 15 minutes.

Remove the pears and citrus slices from the pan, using a slotted spoon and place in a large bowl. Boil the cooking liquid rapidly to reduce to a thin syrup, then pour over the fruit. Leave to cool, then chill in the refrigerator for 1 hour (or longer for a deeper rose colour).

For the citrus crème, simply whisk the ingredients together to a piping consistency. Chill until required.

To make the gingered butterscotch sauce, put the water, liquid glucose and sugar in a small heavy-based pan and dissolve over a low heat. Bring to the boil and cook over a medium heat until a dark caramel is formed. Immediately remove from the heat and carefully add the lime juice, cream and ginger. Return to the heat and bring back to boil. Cook over a high heat for 2 minutes, stirring until thoroughly blended. Strain the sauce through a conical sieve into a jug and leave to cool. The sauce can be served cold or reheated before serving if preferred.

Remove the citrus slices from the syrup and finely pare some of the rind; cut small diamonds and set aside for the decoration.

To serve, drain the pears and thinly slice 4 halves. Trim the other 4 pear halves into nearer circles and place one in the centre of each serving plate. Fan the pear slices around, to resemble the brim of 'the hat'. Pipe citrus crème around the edge to create a ribbon trim effect. Decorate with the citrus diamonds and place a dill or mint sprig in the centre for the 'hat feather'. Spoon the gingered butterscotch sauce between the fanned pear slices. Serve at room temperature, or chilled if preferred.

Note: The quantity of gingered butterscotch sauce is generous! Any leftover sauce can be stored in the refrigerator for up to 3 days.

THE EAST

CONNIE STEVENS • KATINA BEALE • SARAH DYSON

PANEL OF JUDGES
Pat McDonald • Rick Wakeman • Loyd Grossman

KATINA BEALE'S MENU

STARTER
Red Pepper Cream,
with Marinated Roasted Peppers

MAIN COURSE
Little Gâteaux of Aubergine and Almond Polenta
with Basil and Mozzarella, accompanied by
a Thyme and Tomato Concasse

"A winning combination" **Loyd**

Vegetables in Season

DESSERT
Tropical Fruit and Vanilla Ice,
with Peaches, Mango and Paw Paw

K atina Beale comes from Walgrave in Northamptonshire. Katina works in the heady world of advertising: she's the managing director's secretary and general factotum at a busy agency in Northampton. Aromatherapy helps her to relax and cope with the pressure of it all! Katina was this year's only successful vegetarian contestant from the cook-offs.

Red Pepper Cream with Marinated Roasted Peppers

If you have time, prepare the roasted peppers a day ahead and leave to marinate overnight before serving.

Roasted Peppers:
2 yellow peppers
1 red pepper
large pinch of dried herbes de Provençe
1 clove garlic, crushed
about 90 ml (6 tbsp) olive oil

Red Pepper Cream:
15 ml (1 tbsp) olive oil
1 shallot, finely chopped
2 red peppers, deseeded and chopped
1 tomato, skinned and chopped
5 ml (1 tsp) salt
1.25 ml (¼ tsp) cayenne pepper
¾ envelope of gelatine
15 ml (1 tbsp) raspberry vinegar
2.5 ml (½ tsp) raspberry liqueur
10 ml (2 tsp) blackberry liqueur
125 g (4 oz) curd cheese

To prepare the roasted peppers, roast the whole peppers in a preheated oven at 220°C (425°F) mark 7 for about 20 minutes, until charred and blistered all over. Cover and leave until cool enough to handle, then peel away the skins. Cut the flesh into strips, discarding the core and seeds. Place the pepper strips in a shallow dish, add the herbs, garlic and olive oil, turn to coat, then leave to marinate for several hours, or overnight if possible.

To make the red pepper cream, heat the olive oil in a large saucepan, add the chopped shallot and sauté for 1 minute. Add the chopped peppers, tomato, salt and cayenne pepper. Cook over a high heat, stirring to prevent sticking, for 6-7 minutes.

Transfer the mixture to a blender or food processor and work to a purée, then return to a saucepan and cook for about 5 minutes, stirring constantly. Meanwhile, soften the gelatine in 30 ml (2 tbsp) water, then place over a pan of simmering water to dissolve. Stir the dissolved gelatine into the pepper mixture, then pass through a sieve. Allow to cool slightly.

Mix the raspberry vinegar and raspberry liqueur together in a small pan and reduce to 15 ml (1 tbsp) over a high heat – be careful not to completely reduce it to nothing! Stir into the pepper purée with the blackberry liqueur. Leave to cool completely, then mix with the curd cheese. Chill in the refrigerator for at least 2 hours before serving.

Drain the roasted peppers from the marinade and serve with the red pepper cream. Accompany with some olive bread or rustic walnut bread.

LITTLE GATEAUX OF AUBERGINE AND ALMOND POLENTA

4 small plump aubergines
salt and freshly ground black pepper
basil oil, for frying
2 large marjoram sprigs, leaves only
handful of basil leaves, shredded
200 g (7 oz) mozzarella cheese, sliced

Polenta:
1 litre (1¾ pints) water
200 g (7 oz) polenta flour
125 g (4 oz) ground almonds
50 g (2 oz) butter
pinch of freshly grated nutmeg

Thyme and Tomato Concasse:
15 ml (1 tbsp) olive oil
1 shallot, finely chopped
1 clove garlic, crushed
450 g (1 lb) tomatoes, skinned
8 sun-dried tomatoes
15 ml (1 tbsp) tomato purée
2 thyme sprigs
1 glass sweet dessert wine

To Garnish:
basil, marjoram and thyme sprigs

Cut the aubergines into 5 mm (¼ inch) slices, to give 16 rounds. Sprinkle liberally with salt, layer in a colander and leave for about 20 minutes to degorge the bitter juices. Rinse thoroughly, drain and pat dry with kitchen paper.

Meanwhile make the polenta. Bring the water to the boil in a large saucepan, with 1.25 ml (¼ tsp) salt added. Whisk in the polenta flour and simmer, stirring, for 25 minutes or until the mixture leaves the sides of the pan clean. Remove from the heat and add the ground almonds, butter, nutmeg and salt and pepper to taste. Beat thoroughly, using a hand-held electric mixer, or food processor until smooth.

Spread the polenta in an oiled shallow baking tin to a depth of 1 cm (½ inch) and leave to cool. When cold, cut into rounds, the same size as the aubergine slices.

To make the thyme and tomato concasse, heat the oil in a saucepan, add the shallot and garlic and cook gently for 5 minutes until softened. Meanwhile, chop the fresh tomatoes. In a food processor or blender, purée the sun-dried tomatoes with the tomato purée to a smooth paste. Add to the saucepan with the chopped tomatoes, thyme sprigs and wine. Cook very slowly over a low heat, stirring occasionally, for about 45 minutes until thickened, removing the thyme sprigs after 30 minutes. If necessary, add a little water or extra wine to ensure the concasse does not dry out.

Heat 60 ml (4 tbsp) basil oil in a frying pan and sauté the aubergine slices with a few marjoram leaves, in batches, until lightly browned on both sides. Add more oil to the pan as necessary.

To assemble the gâteaux, place 8 aubergine slices in a single layer in an oiled baking dish. Spread a spoonful of tomato concasse on each one, then top with shredded basil and marjoram. Cover with a slice of mozzarella, then a polenta round. Repeat the layers of concasse, herbs and mozzarella. Cover with the remaining aubergine slices, a sprinkling of basil and, finally, mozzarella slices.

Bake in a preheated oven at 180°C (350°F) mark 4 for 20-25 minutes until the cheese is golden brown and bubbling.

Place two aubergine gâteaux in the centre of each warmed serving plate. Pour a little tomato concasse onto each plate and garnish with basil, marjoram and thyme.

TROPICAL FRUIT AND VANILLA ICE, WITH PEACHES, MANGO AND PAW PAW

125 g (4 oz) sugar
juice and finely pared rind of 1 lime
2 paw paws
4 peaches
2 mangoes
15 ml (1 tbsp) vanilla extract (not essence)
400 ml (14 fl oz) crème fraîche
peach liqueur or cointreau, to taste

To Serve:
diced paw paw
mango and peach slices

First prepare the sugar syrup. In a heavy-based pan over a low heat, dissolve the sugar in 300 ml (½ pint) water, with the lime juice and rind added. Increase the heat and boil steadily for 5 minutes. Allow to cool, then strain and reserve 60 ml (2 fl oz).

Halve and peel the paw paws, then scoop out the seeds. Peel, halve and stone the peaches. Peel the mangoes and cut the flesh away from the stone. Cut all the fruit into large chunks.

Put the fruit, cooled syrup and vanilla extract in a blender or food processor and work to a smooth cream. Add the crème fraîche and peach liqueur to taste.

Transfer the mixture to an ice-cream maker and churn for 25 minutes. Transfer to a freezer container and freeze (unless eating straight away). If you do not have an ice-cream maker, freeze in a suitable container, whisking two or three times during freezing to break down the ice crystals and ensure a smooth result.

Ten minutes before serving, transfer the ice cream to the refrigerator to soften. Serve accompanied by diced paw paw, and mango and peach slices.

Note: The quantity of ice cream is sufficient to serve 6-8.

THE EAST

CONNIE STEVENS • KATINA BEALE • SARAH DYSON

PANEL OF JUDGES
Pat McDonald • Rick Wakeman • Loyd Grossman

SARAH DYSON'S MENU

STARTER

Tarragon Mushrooms with Mixed Leaves,
tossed in a Pistachio Dressing

"The way the tarragon came through was very, very good" **Pat McDonald**

MAIN COURSE

Duck Breast with Basil and Lemon,
served on a Potato Rösti with a Mediterranean Salsa

Braised Leeks

Carrots

DESSERT

Collapsed Chocolate Soufflé
with Brandied Berries and Almond Crème Fraîche

S arah Dyson, from North Ormsby in Lincolnshire, is a Human
Resources Manager with an electrical retailer. A keen rider,
Sarah enjoys spending some of her weekends helping at nearby stables
with riding for the disabled. She also likes hunting for antiques and
paintings to grace her cottage.

TARRAGON MUSHROOMS WITH MIXED LEAVES, TOSSED IN A PISTACHIO DRESSING

Use a mixture of cultivated and wild mushrooms for this starter if possible. For optimum effect, choose a colourful selection of salad leaves.

225 g (8 oz) mushrooms
olive oil, for sprinkling
handful of tarragon leaves, chopped
2 eggs
300 ml (½ pint) mixed double cream and
  Greek-style yogurt
salt and freshly ground black pepper
freshly grated nutmeg

To Serve:
assorted salad leaves, eg frisée, oakleaf
  lettuce and lamb's lettuce

Pistachio Dressing:
50 g (2 oz) shelled pistachio nuts
15 ml (1 tbsp) olive oil
juice of ½ lemon
salt and freshly ground black pepper
freshly grated nutmeg

Slice the mushrooms and divide between 4 oiled individual ovenproof dishes. Sprinkle with a little oil, and the chopped tarragon.

In a bowl, beat the eggs with the cream and yogurt mixture. Season with salt, pepper and nutmeg. Pour the mixture over the mushrooms and cook in a preheated oven at 150°C (300°F) mark 2 for about 20 minutes or until set.

Meanwhile combine the salad leaves in a bowl. For the dressing, crush the pistachios and mix with the olive oil and lemon juice. Season with salt, pepper and nutmeg to taste.

Just before serving, toss the leaves in the dressing. Serve the warm tarragon mushrooms with the salad.

DUCK BREAST WITH BASIL AND LEMON, AND POTATO RÖSTI WITH MEDITERRANEAN SALSA

3 duck breasts, skinned
45 ml (3 tbsp) olive oil
juice of 1 lemon
15 ml (1 tbsp) chopped basil
salt and freshly ground black pepper
a little olive oil, for frying

Salsa:
4 baby sweet peppers, cored and seeded
3 sun-dried tomatoes
few green olives, stoned
1 large clove garlic, peeled
finely grated rind of 1 lemon
45 ml (3 tbsp) set yogurt

Rosti:
2 baking potatoes
30 ml (2 tbsp) melted butter

Put the duck breasts in a shallow dish with the olive oil, lemon juice and basil. Turn to coat, then leave to marinate for 1½-2 hours.

To prepare the salsa, chop the peppers, sun-dried tomatoes, olives and garlic. Place in a bowl with the lemon rind and yogurt. Mix well and season with salt and pepper to taste. Set aside.

Peel and grate the potatoes for the rösti. Dry in a tea-towel to remove excess moisture, then place in a bowl. Stir in the melted butter and season liberally with salt and pepper. Divide the mixture into 4 portions.

Heat a large heavy-based frying pan until it is very hot. Add the rosti, pressing each one into a flat round cake, using the back of a fish slice. Cook for about 5 minutes until golden brown underneath, then turn the rösti and cook the other side until crisp and golden brown. Transfer to a warmed plate and keep hot in a warm oven.

Meanwhile, remove the duck breasts from the marinade. Heat a little olive oil in a heavy-based frying pan, add the duck breasts, skin-side down, and fry over a moderate heat for 6-8 minutes. Turn the duck breasts over, lower the heat and cook for 6-8 minutes until tender but still pink inside. Remove from the pan, wrap in foil and leave to rest for 5 minutes.

To serve, carve the duck breasts crosswise into thick slices. Place a rösti in the centre of each warmed serving plate and arrange the slices of duck around the edge. Spoon the salsa on top of the rosti. Serve at once, accompanied by braised leeks and carrots.

Collapsed Chocolate Soufflé with Brandied Berries and Almond Crème Fraîche

Brandied Berries:
175 g (6 oz) mixed berry fruits (eg strawberries, raspberries and blueberries)
15 ml (1 tbsp) caster sugar
45 ml (3 tbsp) brandy

Chocolate Soufflé:
225 g (8 oz) bitter chocolate, in pieces
125 g (4 oz) butter
4 eggs (size 2), separated
125 g (4 oz) caster sugar
15 ml (1 tbsp) amaretto di Saronno liqueur

Almond Crème Fraîche:
150 ml (¼ pint) crème fraîche
15 ml (1 tbsp) amaretto di Saronno liqueur

Put the berry fruits in a bowl and sprinkle with the sugar and brandy. Leave to macerate for several hours, turning occasionally.

For the soufflé, line a 20 cm (8 inch) spring-release cake tin with non-stick baking parchment.

Melt the chocolate with the butter in a heatproof bowl over a pan of hot water. (The water must not boil.)

Beat the egg yolks and sugar together until light and foamy. Beat in the melted chocolate mixture, together with the liqueur.

In another bowl, whisk the egg whites until they form soft peaks, then fold into the chocolate mixture.

Turn into the prepared cake tin and bake in a preheated oven at 170°C (325°F) mark 3 for 30 minutes or until risen and beginning to brown. Allow to cool completely in the tin. For the almond crème fraîche, simply mix the crème fraîche with the liqueur. Chill until required.

To serve, turn out the soufflé and cut into wedges. Serve dusted with icing sugar and accompanied by the brandied berries and almond crème fraîche.

LONDON

FIONA PHELPS • DAVID CHAPMAN • CLAIRE HUDSON

PANEL OF JUDGES

Rowley Leigh • Charles Kennedy • Loyd Grossman

WINNER

FIONA PHELPS' MENU

STARTER

Timbale of Crab with Herbs in a Dill-Scented Sauce

MAIN COURSE

Roast Breast of Duck with a Blackcurrant Sauce

Carrot and Coriander Mousse

Sautéed Potatoes with Garlic

Steamed French Bean Parcels

"Excellent" **Rowley Leigh**

DESSERT

Poached Pears in Shortbread
with a Caramel Sauce and Raspberry Coulis

"Melted on the tongue" **Charles Kennedy**

Fiona Phelps has recently married and lives in North London with her husband Andrew. Together they run their own business, working as tree surgeons. Fiona's hobby is furniture restoration, an interest she shares with her father.

TIMBALE OF CRAB WITH HERBS IN A DILL-SCENTED SAUCE

Timbales:

125 g (4 oz) firm white fish fillet, eg brill or turbot, skinned
salt and freshly ground white pepper
1 egg white
60 ml (2 fl oz) double cream
15 ml (1 tbsp) dry sherry
freshly grated nutmeg, to taste
few chervil leaves
few tiny dill sprigs
225 g (8 oz) crabmeat
8-12 fine asparagus spears

Sauce:

300 ml (½ pint) fish stock
90 ml (3 fl oz) dry sherry
90 ml (3 fl oz) double cream
15 ml (1 tbsp) chopped chervil
15 ml (1 tbsp) chopped dill
125 g (4 oz) unsalted butter, chilled and diced

To prepare the fish mousse, trim the fish, cut into chunks and work in a blender or food processor until smooth. With the machine running, add a pinch of salt and the egg white through the feeder tube; process briefly until the mixture stiffens. Transfer to a bowl and gradually beat in two thirds of the cream. Stir in the 15 ml (1 tbsp) sherry and season with salt, pepper and nutmeg to taste. Cover and chill in the refrigerator.

Butter 4 individual moulds and press a few chervil leaves and dill sprigs onto the base of each one.

For the sauce, combine the fish stock and sherry in a saucepan and boil until reduced by three quarters.

Season the crabmeat with salt and pepper to taste, then mix with the fish mousse. The mixture should be just firm enough to hold its shape; if too firm add more of the cream; if too soft, chill for longer. Divide the fish mixture between the moulds, packing it well down, and cover each one with buttered foil.

Stand the moulds on a sheet of greaseproof paper in a bain-marie or roasting tin containing enough boiling water to come halfway up the sides of the moulds. Bake in a preheated oven at 200°C (400°F) mark 6 for 15 minutes.

Meanwhile, trim and peel the asparagus, then steam or cook in boiling salted water for 2 minutes. Drain.

To finish the sauce, stir in the cream, then gradually add the butter a piece at a time, whisking constantly on and off the heat. Stir in the chervil and dill.

To serve, turn each mousse out onto a warmed serving plate. Surround with the sauce and asparagus. Serve at once.

Skewered Fish with Risotto
PETER ANDERSON'S MAIN COURSE (Semi-Final)

Macadamia and Sesame Chicken on Thai-style Salad
ALISON FIANDER'S STARTER (Semi-Final)

ROAST BREAST OF DUCK WITH A BLACKCURRANT SAUCE

3 duck breasts
sea salt and freshly ground black pepper
30 ml (2 tbsp) redcurrant jelly
600 ml (1 pint) duck or brown stock
300 ml (½ pint) red wine
125 ml (4 fl oz) port
1 thyme sprig
1 rosemary sprig
75 g (3 oz) blackcurrants
5 ml (1 tsp) arrowroot, blended with 5 ml
    (1 tsp) water

Score the fat on the duck breasts, then rub with salt and spread thinly with half of the redcurrant jelly.

To make the sauce, pour the stock and red wine into a saucepan and boil to reduce by two thirds. Add the port, herbs, blackcurrants and remaining redcurrant jelly and allow to simmer until reduced by half. Strain, then reheat and adjust the seasoning. Stir in the arrowroot paste and cook, stirring, for about 1 minute, until thickened and clear; keep warm.

To cook the duck breasts, preheat a heavy-based frying pan. When it is very hot add the duck breasts, skin-side down, and fry for 3 minutes. Turn and cook the other side for 1 minute to sear. Transfer, skin-side up, to a rack over a roasting tin and cook in a preheated oven at 200°C (400°F) mark 6 for 10 minutes.

To serve, carve the duck breasts into slices. Arrange around a carrot mousse on each warmed serving plate. Pour the sauce over the meat and serve at once, with sautéed potatoes and steamed French beans.

CARROT AND CORIANDER MOUSSE

450 g (1 lb) carrots, peeled and chopped
300 ml (½ pint) chicken stock
5 ml (1 tbsp) chopped coriander leaves
15 ml (1 tbsp) crème fraîche
25 g (1 oz) butter, melted
1 egg
salt and freshly ground black pepper
freshly grated nutmeg

Cook the carrots in the chicken stock until soft. Drain and place in a food processor or blender with the coriander, crème fraîche and melted butter. Work to a purée. Whisk the egg in a bowl, then fold into the carrot purée. Season with salt, pepper and nutmeg to taste.

Divide the carrot mousse between 4 oiled dariole moulds, packing it well down. Cover the moulds with oiled rounds of foil. Stand in a bain-marie or roasting tin lined with greaseproof paper and pour in sufficient hot water to come halfway up the sides of the moulds.

Bake on the middle shelf of a preheated oven at 200°C (400°F) mark 6 for 20-25 minutes. Leave to stand in the bain-marie for 5 minutes, then turn out onto warmed plates to serve.

POACHED PEARS IN SHORTBREAD LAYERS WITH A CARAMEL SAUCE AND RASPBERRY COULIS

Shortbread Pastry:
250 g (9 oz) plain flour
pinch of baking powder
pinch of salt
2 egg yolks
30 ml (2 tbsp) whipping cream
85 g (3¼ oz) icing sugar
dash of vanilla essence
175 g (6 oz) butter, softened

Poached Pears:
2 firm, ripe pears (preferably William)
finely pared rind and juice of 1 lemon
150 g (5 oz) caster sugar
400 ml (14 fl oz) water
½ vanilla pod, split
1 cinnamon stick

Caramel Sauce:
125 g (4 oz) caster sugar
60 ml (2 fl oz) water
200 ml (7 fl oz) double cream
50 g (2 oz) unsalted butter
juice of 1 lime

Raspberry Coulis:
125 g (4 oz) fresh or frozen raspberries
lemon juice, to taste
icing sugar, to taste

To Assemble:
120 ml (4 oz) double cream, whipped
icing sugar, for dusting

To make the shortbread pastry, sift the flour, baking powder and salt onto a work surface and make a well in the centre. In a bowl, beat the egg yolks with the cream, icing sugar and vanilla essence, then gradually mix in the butter. Add to the well, and gradually work in the flour. Knead lightly until smooth, then wrap in cling film and leave to rest in the refrigerator for 1 hour.

Roll out the dough on a lightly floured surface to a 3mm (⅛ inch) thickness and cut out twelve 6 cm (2½ inch) rounds. Place on baking sheets and bake in a preheated oven at 180°C (350°F) mark 4 for 5-10 minutes until golden; watch carefully. Transfer to a wire rack to cool.

Meanwhile, peel, halve and core the pears and sprinkle with lemon juice to prevent discolouration. Put the sugar and water into a saucepan with the vanilla, cinnamon and lemon rind. Heat gently until the sugar is dissolved, then add the pears. Cover with a disc of greaseproof paper and simmer gently for 20 minutes.

Meanwhile, make the caramel sauce. Dissolve the sugar in the water in a heavy-based pan, then bring to the boil and cook to a dark caramel. Carefully stir in half of the cream, then remove from the heat and stir in the remaining cream, butter and lime juice, to form a smooth sauce.

To make the raspberry coulis, gently heat the raspberries in a saucepan for 30 seconds, then purée in a blender or food processor, with a little water if necessary. Pass through a sieve and add lemon juice and icing sugar to taste.

Remove the pears from the syrup with a slotted spoon and slice thinly. Layer up the shortbread pastry rounds, sandwiching them together in threes with the pears and whipped cream. Dust the tops with icing sugar and place on individual serving plates. Spoon the caramel sauce around one side of the biscuits; pour the raspberry coulis around the other side. Serve at once.

LONDON

FIONA PHELPS • DAVID CHAPMAN • CLAIRE HUDSON

PANEL OF JUDGES
Rowley Leigh • Charles Kennedy • Loyd Grossman

DAVID CHAPMAN'S MENU

STARTER

Tataki (Seared Tuna Sashimi)
with Japanese-style Condiments

"Terrific" **Charles Kennedy**

MAIN COURSE

Pan-fried Calves Liver
with Grilled Pineapple

Caesar Salad

DESSERT

Chocolate Bread and Butter Pudding

"Intriguing" **Charles Kennedy**

D avid Chapman lives near the City in a flat overlooking
the Thames. As an equity sales manager with a Japanese
Bank, he is an expert in stocks and shares. David is also a horse
racing enthusiast and part-owns a two year old race horse,
called 'Young at Heart'.

TATAKI (SEARED TUNA SASHIMI) WITH JAPANESE-STYLE CONDIMENTS

For this starter, you will need to prepare the lemon soy sauce a day in advance to allow time for the flavours to be absorbed.

700 g (1½ lb) very fresh tuna
salt and freshly ground black pepper
few drops of extra-virgin olive oil
lemon juice, for sprinkling

Lemon Soy Sauce:
105 ml (7 tbsp) lemon juice
105 ml (7 tbsp) dark soy sauce
25 ml (5 tsp) rice wine vinegar
25 ml (5 tsp) mirin
7 g (¼ oz) dried bonito flakes

Condiments:
1 head of chicory
20 basil leaves
4 spring onions, finely chopped
60 ml (4 tbsp) finely chopped fresh root
  ginger

To Garnish:
pickled ginger
enoki mushrooms (uncooked)

To prepare the lemon soy sauce, combine the lemon juice, soy sauce, rice wine vinegar, mirin and bonito flakes in a bowl. Cover and refrigerate for 24 hours. Strain before serving.

Season the tuna with salt and pepper. Oil a skillet or heavy-based frying pan with a few drops of olive oil and place over a high heat. When it is very hot, add the tuna and sear on all sides, ensuring the fish remains uncooked in the centre. Immediately immerse the tuna in ice-cold water to refresh. Drain when cool and pat dry with absorbent kitchen paper. Cut the fish into 1 cm (½ inch) slices. Sprinkle with lemon juice, cover and refrigerate for at least 1 hour.

Meanwhile prepare the condiments. Finely chop the chicory and basil leaves. Mix with the spring onions and ginger.

To serve, divide the tuna between 4 serving plates. Pat with the condiments. Garnish with pickled ginger and enoki mushrooms. Provide each guest with a small dish of lemon soy sauce for dipping.

Note: Dried Bonito flakes are an essential ingredient in Japanese marinades and stocks. They are available from specialist shops and may be described as *hana-katsuo*.

PAN-FRIED CALVES LIVER WITH GRILLED PINEAPPLE

1 small pineapple
125 ml (4 fl oz) plum wine
125 ml (4 fl oz) Japanese rice wine vinegar
10 ml (2 tsp) olive oil
5 ml (1 tsp) unsalted butter
700 g (1½ lb) calves liver
flour, for coating

Sauce:
125 ml (4 fl oz) red wine
125 ml (4 fl oz) port
30 ml (2 tbsp) rice vinegar
60 ml (¼ cup) veal stock
50 g (2 oz) chilled unsalted butter, in pieces
large pinch of ground cinnamon
salt and freshly ground black pepper

To Garnish:
16 chives, with flowers if possible
5 ml (1 tsp) jalapeno peppers, chopped
  (optional)

Cut the top and base off the pineapple, then cut away the skin and remove the brown 'eyes'. Cut four 1 cm (½ inch) slices from the centre of the pineapple; chop the rest, discarding the hard central core and set aside 125 g (4 oz) for the garnish. Combine the plum wine and rice vinegar in a shallow dish. Add the pineapple rings, turn to coat with the mixture and leave to marinate for 15 minutes.

Meanwhile prepare the sauce. Put the red wine, port and rice vinegar in a small pan and boil until reduced by half. Add the veal stock and boil to reduce until the sauce starts to thicken. Whisk in the butter, cinnamon and salt and pepper to taste until smooth. Keep warm.

Drain the pineapple rings and cook under a preheated hot grill, turning occasionally, until golden brown on both sides. Meanwhile cut the liver into 5 mm (¼ inch) thick slices – to give 2-3 slices per serving. Drizzle with a little olive oil. Toss in flour to coat evenly. Heat the butter and remaining olive oil in a heavy-based frying pan. When it is very hot, add the liver slices and sauté over a high heat for no longer than 1 minute each side.

To serve, toss the chopped fresh pineapple in the sauce. Arrange the liver slices and grilled pineapple slices on warmed serving plates. Garnish with the chives, and peppers if using. Serve with the sauce.

Caesar Salad

2 small gem lettuces, trimmed
50 g (1¾ oz) can anchovies, drained

Garlic Croûtons:
4 thick slices white bread, crusts removed
30-45 ml (2-3 tbsp) olive oil
2 cloves garlic, crushed
50 g (2 oz) Parmesan cheese, freshly grated

Dressing:
1 egg yolk
1 clove garlic
60 ml (2 fl oz) sherry vinegar
120 ml (4 fl oz) olive oil
dash of Worcestershire Sauce

To Serve:
finely pared or grated Parmesan cheese

Slice the lettuces crosswise and place in a salad bowl. Cut the anchovies into small pieces.

To prepare the croûtons, cut the bread into small cubes. Heat the olive oil in a frying pan with the crushed garlic. Add the bread cubes and fry until golden brown. Drain on absorbent kitchen paper and allow to cool. Add the croûtons to the lettuce with the anchovies and Parmesan and toss lightly.

Combine the ingredients for the dressing in a screw-topped jar and shake vigorously to emulsify. Toss the salad with the dressing and top with Parmesan to taste. Serve at once.

Chocolate Bread and Butter Pudding

75 g (3 oz) dried cherries, dried cranberries or sultanas
125 ml (4 fl oz) cognac
1½ brioche loaves, crusts removed
225 g (8 oz) quality dark chocolate, in pieces
3 eggs
250 ml (8 fl oz) double cream
125 ml (4 fl oz) soured cream
125 g (4 oz) sugar
pinches of ground cinnamon
5 ml (1 tsp) vanilla extract

To Serve:
250 ml (8 fl oz) crème fraîche
15 ml (1 tbsp) caster sugar

Put the dried cherries, cranberries or sultanas in a bowl. Pour on the cognac and leave to soak for at least 1 hour. Cut the brioche into small cubes and lightly toast, turning until evenly golden brown on all sides; set aside.

Melt the chocolate in a heatproof bowl over a pan of hot water; stir until smooth. Allow to cool slightly. In a large bowl, beat the eggs with the creams, sugar, cinnamon, vanilla and melted chocolate. Add the toasted bread cubes, soaked fruit and any remaining cognac. Set this mixture aside for 1½ hours to allow the bread to absorb the mixture.

Butter 4 ramekins and fill with the pudding mixture. Stand the ramekins in a bain-marie or roasting tin containing enough hot water to come halfway up the sides. Bake in a preheated oven at 170°C (325°F) mark 3 for 35 minutes. Meanwhile whip the crème fraîche lightly with the caster sugar.

Serve the pudding warm, accompanied by the crème fraîche.

LONDON

FIONA PHELPS • DAVID CHAPMAN • CLAIRE HUDSON

PANEL OF JUDGES
Rowley Leigh • Charles Kennedy • Loyd Grossman

CLAIRE HUDSON'S MENU

STARTER
Thai Melon Salad
with Smoked Breast of Duck
"Very Original" **Rowley Leigh**

MAIN COURSE
Salmon with Sorrel
Gratins Daupinoise
Vegetable 'Noodles'

DESSERT
Brown Bread Ice Cream
with a Compote of Caramelised Oranges
"Pretty well ace" **Rowley Leigh**

C laire Hudson, from Chingford in Essex, is the Librarian at London's Theatre Museum in Covent Garden where she researches into Britain's theatrical heritage. Claire is an avid collector of period cookery books, and her collection extends to 700 or so. To relax and get away from it all, Claire enjoys leisurely bike rides with her husband, Stephen, in Epping Forest.

THAI MELON SALAD WITH SMOKED BREAST OF DUCK

Infusion:
125 g (4 oz) sugar
150 ml (¼ pint) water
1 green chilli, deseeded and roughly chopped
2 lemon grass stalks
3 kaffir lime leaves
2.5 cm (1 inch) piece of root ginger, peeled
 and sliced

Smoked Duck:
2 boneless breasts of duck
45 ml (3 tbsp) dry oolong tea
45 ml (3 tbsp) white rice
30 ml (2 tbsp) sugar

Melon Salad:
1 cantaloupe melon
25 g (1 oz) dark-roasted unsalted peanuts
1 dried red chilli, deseeded and finely
 chopped
2.5 ml (½ tsp) salt
5 ml (1 tsp) sugar

To Garnish:
coriander sprigs

To make the infusion, dissolve the sugar in the water in a saucepan over a low heat. Add the green chilli, lemon grass, lime leaves and ginger. Bring to the boil, then lower the heat and simmer for 10 minutes. Taste and remove the chilli at this stage if the infusion is sufficiently fiery for your taste. Allow to cool, then chill in the refrigerator. Strain the infusion before use.

To prepare the duck, place a double layer of foil in the bottom of a wok with a lid. Sprinkle the tea, rice and sugar over the foil. Stand a rack over the top, well clear of the tea mixture. Lay the duck breasts on the rack, skin-side up. Place the lid on the wok and seal well with foil.

Place over a high heat for 4 minutes, then lower the heat to medium for a further 3 minutes. Turn off the heat but leave the duck undisturbed to continue smoking for at least 30 minutes. Remove from the wok and chill before serving.

Just before serving, halve the melon and scoop out the seeds. Cut into slices and remove the skin. Finely slice the duck breasts. Arrange the melon and duck slices separately on each serving plate. Chop the peanuts and mix with the red chilli, salt and sugar. Dress the melon with a little of the infusion and a sprinkling of the peanut mixture. Garnish with coriander sprigs.

SALMON WITH SORREL

15 ml (1 tbsp) oil
25 g (1 oz) butter
4 salmon fillets, each about 175 g (6 oz)
salt and freshly ground black pepper

Sauce:
300 ml (½ pint) fish stock
120 ml (4 fl oz) white wine
150 ml (¼ pint) double cream
50 g (2 oz) sorrel leaves
25 g (1 oz) butter, in pieces, chilled
squeeze of lemon juice

First make the sauce. Pour the stock and wine into a saucepan and reduce over a medium heat until syrupy. Add the cream and boil down until reduced and thickened. Meanwhile, tear the sorrel leaves into pieces, removing the central midrib. Add the sorrel pieces to the sauce – they will immediately cook down. Add the butter and swirl the pan until the butter is incorporated into the sauce. Sharpen the sauce slightly with a little lemon juice; season with salt only if needed. Keep warm.

To cook the salmon, heat the oil in a sauté pan. Add the butter and, when the foaming subsides, add the salmon fillets. Fry for about 4 minutes each side, depending on the thickness of the fillets.

To serve, pour a small pool of sauce onto each warmed serving plate. Position a salmon fillet on top and sprinkle with a little salt and pepper. Serve at once, with the accompaniments.

Note: This recipe has been adapted from one by Ian McAndrew, in '*A Feast of Fish*' (published 1987).

GRATINS DAUPINOISE

50 g (2 oz) butter
1 clove garlic, crushed
2.5 ml (½ tsp) powdered mace
900 g (2 lb) small potatoes
salt and freshly ground black pepper
120 ml (4 fl oz) single cream

Melt the butter in a small pan and add the garlic and mace. Turn off the heat and allow the flavours to develop while you prepare the potatoes.

Peel the potatoes and slice thinly, using a food processor or mandoline set to a fine cut. Brush 4 ramekins liberally with the flavoured butter. Lay two double strips of greaseproof paper crosswise in each ramekin allowing them to overhang the edge – these will help in turning out the gratins after cooking. Brush with the flavoured butter.

Layer the sliced potatoes in the ramekins, sprinkling each layer with butter and salt and pepper. Carefully pour a little of the cream into each dish. Cook in a preheated oven at 170°C (325°F) mark 3 for 1¼ hours or until the potatoes are tender.

To serve, loosen the gratins by working a knife around the side of each ramekin. Use the paper strips to help release the gratins and transfer to the warmed serving plates.

Note: Alternatively the gratins can be partially cooked in the microwave, in which case you will only need half of the quantity of cream. Cover the dishes with cling film and pierce to allow steam to escape. Microwave on HIGH for 10 minutes, then remove the film and place in a preheated oven at 200°C (400°F) mark 6 for about 25 minutes until browned.

Vegetable 'Noodles'

½ cucumber
450 g (1 lb) straight carrots, peeled
1 red pepper
25 g (1 oz) butter
10 ml (2 tsp) sugar
salt and freshly ground black pepper
15 ml (1 tbsp) balsamic vinegar

Halve the cucumber lengthwise and scoop out the watery seed centre. Cut lengthwise into fine slices, then into 3 mm (⅛ inch) wide strips. Cut the carrots lengthwise into similar-sized strips.

Halve the red pepper lengthwise and remove the core and seeds. Place cut-side down under a preheated hot grill until charred. Cover with a damp cloth. When cool, peel and cut the pepper lengthwise into fine strips.

Melt the butter in a saucepan and add the carrots, sugar and seasoning. Cover and cook gently for 4 minutes. Add the remaining vegetables and cover tightly to steam for 2 minutes. Add the balsamic vinegar. Increase the heat and reduce the cooking juices to a syrupy dressing. Serve immediately.

Brown Bread Ice Cream with a Compote of Caramelised Oranges

Ice Cream:
125 g (4 oz) fresh wholemeal breadcrumbs
50 g (2 oz) light muscovado sugar
2 eggs, separated
60 ml (2 fl oz) Baileys liqueur
300 ml (½ pint) double cream
50 g (2 oz) caster sugar

Orange Compote:
4 oranges
50 g (2 oz) sugar
120 ml (4 fl oz) orange juice

Spread out the breadcrumbs on a baking tray and cover with the muscovado sugar. Place near the top of a preheated oven at 190°C (375°F) mark 5 to toast, checking after 10 minutes and thereafter every 5 minutes, stirring each time to ensure even browning. After 25 minutes the crumbs should be deep brown and crisp, and the sugar beginning to caramelise. Leave to cool, then chill.

Mix the egg yolks with the liqueur. Whip the cream until soft peaks form, then fold in the egg yolk mixture. In a separate bowl, whisk the egg whites until stiff, then gradually whisk in the caster sugar to form a shiny meringue. Fold into the ice cream base, then carefully fold in the toasted crumbs.

Freeze in an ice cream machine until thick and well chilled, then transfer to individual freezerproof moulds (or one large one) and freeze until firm.

Meanwhile, prepare the compote. Using a sharp knife, peel the rind and pith from the oranges and divide into neat segments, cutting them free of the membrane. Melt the sugar in a heavy-based pan over a low heat, then increase the heat and cook to a golden caramel. Carefully add the orange juice – the mixture will splutter. Stir over a low heat to dissolve any hard caramel, then increase the heat and reduce the sauce to approximately 60 ml (2 fl oz). Pour the caramel over the orange segments and leave to stand for at least 1 hour before serving.

To serve, unmould the ice cream, (cut into slices if appropriate) and place on chilled serving plates. Spoon a portion of orange compote onto each plate.

Note: If you do not have an ice cream machine, freeze the ice cream in a shallow container until almost firm, whisking periodically to break down the ice crystals. Continue as above.

SEMI-FINAL

ELAINE BATES • PETER ANDERSON • SOPHIE BUCHMANN

PANEL OF JUDGES

Sally Clarke • Alan Yentob • Loyd Grossman

WINNER

ELAINE BATES' MENU

STARTER

Spiced Cornucopia of Wild Mushrooms

"Very, very nice" **Alan Yentob**

MAIN COURSE

*Salmis of Pheasant
with Chestnuts and Redcurrants*

Wild Rice with Lemon Grass

Braised Celery Hearts

DESSERT

*Roasted Figs in Honey Butter and Orange,
served with Orange Sablés*

SPICED CORNUCOPIA OF WILD MUSHROOMS

For this starter, use a mixture of different mushrooms – such as pied de moutons, chanterelles, oyster and button mushrooms – depending on whatever is available.

450 g (1 lb) assorted mushrooms
120 ml (4 fl oz) olive oil
10 ml (2 tsp) cumin seeds
10 ml (2 tsp) coriander seeds
120 ml (4 fl oz) white wine
75 ml (2½ fl oz) water
rosemary sprig
juice of ½ lemon
freshly ground black pepper
30 ml (2 tbsp) chopped coriander leaves
1 clove garlic, crushed
4 thin slices white bread
few salad leaves, to garnish

Clean the mushrooms thoroughly. Heat half of the olive oil in a saucepan, add the cumin and coriander seeds and sauté for 1 minute, then add the mushrooms and sauté for 2 minutes. Add the wine, water, rosemary and lemon juice and simmer for about 10 minutes. Turn up the heat and boil rapidly until the liquid has reduced by half. Season with pepper to taste. Stir in the chopped coriander and keep warm.

To make the cornucopias, mix the remaining olive oil with the garlic. Brush each slice of bread liberally with the garlic oil, then wrap around a cream horn tin and press the edges together, cutting off any excess, to achieve a horn shape. Place on a baking tray and bake in a preheated oven at 180°C (350°F) mark 4 for 10-15 minutes until light golden. Carefully remove the bread horns from the tins.

To serve, spoon some of the mushrooms into each bread horn, then lay on a serving plate. Spoon the rest of the mushrooms onto the plates so that they look as if they are spilling out of the cornucopias. Pour some of the juices from the mushrooms around the plate and garnish with a few salad leaves. Serve at once.

SALMIS OF PHEASANT WITH CHESTNUTS AND REDCURRANTS

2 pheasants
16 fresh chestnuts (or vacuum-packed
* chestnuts)*
175 g (6 oz) unsalted butter
10 ml (2 tsp) sugar
600 ml (1 pint) pheasant stock (see below)
salt and freshly ground black pepper
15 ml (1 tbsp) red wine vinegar
30 ml (2 tbsp) brandy
150 ml (¼ pint) red wine (eg Burgundy)
10 ml (2 tsp) redcurrant jelly
50 g (2 oz) redcurrants

Remove the breasts and wing tips from the pheasants by scraping a knife between the bone and the breast along to the wing, cutting through the bone at the wing end if necessary. Use the carcasses to make the stock (see below).

If using fresh chestnuts, make a slit in their shells, then add to a pan of boiling water and cook for about 30 minutes. Drain and cool slightly, then peel off the shells and skins.

Melt 50 g (2 oz) butter in a non-stick pan, then add the sugar, chestnuts and 60 ml (2 fl oz) pheasant stock. Cook over a very low heat, turning occasionally, until the liquid has almost evaporated and the chestnuts are glazed.

Season the pheasant breasts with salt and pepper. Heat 50 g (2 oz) of the butter in a large pan. Add the pheasant breasts, skin-side down, and cook until golden brown, then turn and brown the underside. Add the wine vinegar, then the brandy and half of the stock. Bring to the boil, reduce the heat and simmer gently for 10-15 minutes, depending on the thickness of the breasts, until just slightly pink in the middle. Remove from the pan and keep warm.

Add the rest of the stock to the pan with the wine and redcurrant jelly and boil rapidly until reduced by half. Whisk in the remaining 50 g (2 oz) butter, a piece at a time, until the sauce is glossy. Stir in the redcurrants.

To serve, cut the pheasant breasts into fine slices, leaving a portion attached to the wing. Fan the slices out on warmed serving plates. Garnish with the chestnuts and spoon plenty of the sauce around. Serve at once, accompanied by the rice and braised celery.

Pheasant Stock: Heat 30 ml (2 tbsp) oil in a large pan and brown the pheasant carcasses. Roughly chop 2 onions and 2 carrots; add these to the pan and brown. Add a sprig of thyme and 600 ml (1 pint) water. Bring to the boil, then lower the heat and simmer for 10 minutes. Add a bottle of full-bodied red wine (eg Burgundy), 5 ml (1 tsp) juniper berries, a bay leaf and a bouquet garni. Bring back to the boil, lower the heat and simmer gently for about 3 hours. At this stage, there should be about 600 ml (1 pint). Strain the stock into a bowl and allow to cool. Refrigerate when cold so that the fat sets on the surface. Remove this before use.

BRAISED CELERY HEARTS

2 heads of celery
5 ml (1 tsp) chopped thyme
salt and freshly ground black pepper

Discard the outer celery stalks, then cut off the top half of the remaining stalks. Halve each celery heart, then place in a single layer in a saucepan. Add sufficient water to cover. Add the thyme and salt and pepper. Cook gently for about 15 minutes; the celery should still be slightly crunchy. Drain and serve.

WILD RICE WITH LEMON GRASS

125 g (4 oz) wild rice
25 g (1 oz) brown rice
2 lemon grass stalks
50 g (2 oz) butter
finely pared rind of 1 lemon
salt and freshly ground black pepper

Bring a large pan of salted water to the boil and add the wild and brown rice. Halve one stalk of lemon grass lengthways, then add to the pan with the rice. Simmer for 40 minutes, or until the rice is tender. Drain well, discarding the lemon grass.

Meanwhile, discard any coarse outer leaves from the other lemon grass stalk and chop very finely. Melt the butter in a pan, add the rice, lemon grass and lemon rind, and mix well. Heat through and keep warm until ready to serve.

ROASTED FIGS IN HONEY BUTTER AND ORANGE

12 fresh figs
50 g (2 oz) unsalted butter
30 ml (2 tbsp) honey
finely grated rind and juice of 1 orange

Orange Cream:
150 ml (¼ pint) double cream
juice of ½ orange

To Serve:
Orange Sablés (see right)

Peel the figs and cut each one vertically into quarters, without cutting right through to the base. Melt the butter and honey in an ovenproof dish, then stir in the orange juice. Place the figs in a single layer in the dish and sprinkle over the orange rind. Cook in a preheated oven at 190°C (375°F) mark 5

for 15 minutes, basting occasionally.

Meanwhile, to make the orange cream, lightly whip the cream with the orange juice.

Place 3 figs on each warmed serving plate and spoon over some of the juices. Serve warm, with the orange cream and accompanied by the orange sablés.

ORANGE SABLÉS

100 g (3 ½ oz) butter
1 egg yolk
110 g (4½ oz) plain flour
50 g (2 oz) icing sugar
finely grated rind of 1 orange
10 ml (2 tsp) orange juice (approximately)

Place all the ingredients, except the orange juice, in a food processor and process quickly until smooth. Add enough of the orange juice to bind the dough. Wrap in cling film and chill in the freezer for 30 minutes.

Roll out the dough on a lightly floured surface to a 5 mm (¼ inch) thickness and cut into 5 cm (2 inch) rounds. Place on a lightly greased baking sheet and bake in a preheated oven at 190°C (375°F) for 6-8 minutes until light golden. Cool on a wire rack.

SEMI-FINAL

ELAINE BATES • PETER ANDERSON • SOPHIE BUCHMANN

PANEL OF JUDGES
Sally Clarke • Alan Yentob • Loyd Grossman

PETER ANDERSON'S MENU

STARTER
Salad of Pig's Cheek with Lentils

MAIN COURSE
Skewered Fish with Risotto

Stewed Cherry Tomatoes

Crispy Cabbage

"The flavours of the risotto were lovely" **Sally Clarke**

DESSERT
Crunchy Caramel Pastry
with Bananas and Orange Juice,
served with Chocolate Sauce

"Delicious" **Sally Clarke**

SALAD OF PIG'S CHEEK WITH LENTILS

1 pig's cheek
1 leek
1 onion, chopped
4 carrots, plus 25 g (1oz)
2 bay leaves
125 g (4 oz) lentils de Puy or brown lentils
1 small beetroot
40 g (1 ½ oz) fresh foie gras
25 g (1 oz) butter
50 g (2 oz) assorted seasonal salad leaves
15 ml (1 tbsp) olive oil
60 ml (2 fl oz) veal stock

Put the pig's cheek into a large saucepan with the leek, onion, the 4 carrots, bay leaves and sufficient water to cover. Bring to the boil, skim the surface, then simmer for 2 hours or until tender. Drain and keep warm.

Meanwhile, add the lentils to a pan of cold salted water, bring to the boil and simmer for 20 minutes or until tender; drain and cool. Cook the 25 g (1 oz) carrot in simmering water for 10 minutes; drain, refresh in cold water, then dice. Bake the beetroot in a preheated oven at 190°C (375°F) mark 5 for 1 hour. Cool, then dice. Chill the lentils, carrot and beetroot until ready to serve.

Cut the foie gras into 4 rounds. Heat the butter in a pan and gently fry the foie gras rounds until lightly browned.

Arrange the salad leaves in the middle of each serving plate and scatter the carrot, beetroot and lentils on top. Mix the olive oil and veal stock together in a saucepan, gently warm through, then drizzle over the salad.

Remove the fat from the pig's cheek and cut into thin slices. Arrange in a pyramid around the salad leaves. Place a slice of foie gras in the centre and serve at once.

SKEWERED FISH

2 swordfish steaks
4 scallops, cleaned
4 large raw tiger prawns
2 courgettes
salt and freshly ground black pepper
lemon juice, for sprinkling
120 ml (4 fl oz) olive oil
125 g (4 oz) butter
50 g (2 oz) fresh root ginger, peeled and cut
    into very fine strips

Cut each swordfish steak into 2 pieces, discarding the bone. Remove the corals from the scallops. Shell the prawns and remove the black intestinal thread.

Pare the courgettes into long paper-thin slices, using a vegetable peeler. Season with salt and pepper and sprinkle with lemon juice. Roll each piece of fish in a slice of courgette and thread onto 4 skewers. Repeat with the scallops and tiger prawns.

Place the 4 skewers in a steamer and steam for 3-5 minutes. Meanwhile heat the oil and butter in a deep frying pan. Add the skewers and shallow-fry for about 5 minutes or until the courgette browns. Drain thoroughly on absorbent kitchen paper. Briefly fry the shredded ginger until crisp and brown.

Serve the fish skewers on a bed of risotto, topped with the ginger.

RISOTTO

15 ml (1 tbsp) olive oil
1 small onion, chopped
2 cloves garlic, chopped
175 g (6 oz) risotto rice (eg Arborio)
450 ml (¾ pint) dry white wine
900 ml (1½ pints) chicken stock
10 ml (2 tsp) salt
2 plum tomatoes, skinned, seeded and diced
125 g (4 oz) unsalted butter, softened
200 g (7 oz) Parmesan cheese, freshly grated
60 ml (4 tbsp) chopped parsley

Heat the oil in a heavy-based pan, add the onion and garlic, and sweat until softened. Add the rice and cook, stirring constantly, for 2 minutes. Add the wine, stirring to deglaze and boil until completely reduced. Meanwhile, bring the chicken stock to the boil in another pan.

Add a ladleful of boiling stock to the rice mixture and cook, stirring constantly, until it is completely absorbed. Continue adding the stock in this way, a ladleful at a time, as each addition is absorbed. When the rice is plump, creamy and tender, but still retains a bite, it is ready; you may not need to add all of the stock. Stir in the salt and tomatoes. Remove from the heat and beat in the butter and Parmesan. Add the chopped parsley and serve.

STEWED CHERRY TOMATOES

20 cherry tomatoes
175 ml (6 fl oz) olive oil
rock salt, for sprinkling

Remove the stalks from the cherry tomatoes, then make a cut in the top of each one.

Place the tomatoes in a roasting tin together with the olive oil. Sprinkle liberally with rock salt and bake in a preheated oven at 170°C (325°F) mark 3 for 30 minutes, basting occasionally with olive oil. Serve hot.

CRISPY CABBAGE

½ white firm cabbage
½ Savoy cabbage
50 g (2 oz) butter
25 g (1 oz) brown sugar
60 ml (2 fl oz) dry gin
60 ml (2 fl oz) olive oil

Thinly slice both cabbages, discarding the core.

Melt the butter with the sugar in a large saucepan over a low heat. Add the sliced cabbage and cook, stirring constantly, for 2 minutes. Add the gin and continue to cook, stirring, until the cabbage has softened slightly.

Heat the oil in a large frying pan or wok. Add the cabbage and stir-fry over a high heat for 5 minutes or until cooked but retaining a bite. Serve at once.

CRUNCHY CARAMEL PASTRY WITH BANANAS, ORANGE JUICE AND CHOCOLATE SAUCE

2 bananas
60 ml (2 fl oz) orange juice
60 ml (2 fl oz) Grand Marnier
225 g (8 oz) ready-made puff pastry
icing sugar, for dusting

Chocolate Sauce:
225 g (8 oz) rich dark chocolate
125 ml (4 fl oz) double cream
   (approximately), at room temperature

Peel the bananas and barely mash with the orange juice and liqueur. Cover and chill in the refrigerator until ice cold.

Roll out the puff pastry on a surface dusted with icing sugar, as thinly as possible. Roll up the pastry into a sausage shape, then cut 12 rounds. Roll out each one as thinly as possible, then trim to a 7.5 cm (3 inch) round. You should be able to see a spiral effect in the pastry.

Place the pastry rounds on baking sheets lined with non-stick baking parchment. Cover with another sheet of parchment and place another baking sheet on top to impede rising. Bake in a preheated oven at 180°C (350°F) mark 4 for 10 minutes or until golden brown. Set aside to cool.

For the chocolate sauce, melt the chocolate in a double boiler or heatproof bowl over a pan of hot water. Stir until smooth, then gradually stir in the cream, until the desired consistency is achieved.

To serve, place a pastry round on each serving plate. Spread a layer of banana mixture on top and repeat the layers. Top with the remaining pastry rounds and dust with icing sugar. Pour the chocolate sauce around the pastries and serve at once.

SEMI-FINAL

ELAINE BATES • PETER ANDERSON • SOPHIE BUCHMANN

PANEL OF JUDGES
Sally Clarke • Alan Yentob • Loyd Grossman

SOPHIE BUCHMANN'S MENU

STARTER
Ravioli 'Las Vegas'

MAIN COURSE
*Pigeon Breast stuffed with Smoked Aubergine
and Pickled Walnuts, served with a Game and Garlic Sauce*

Braised Red Cabbage

Mashed Turnips and Crispy Shallots in Celery Nests

DESSERT
Caramelised Raspberries with a Lemon Posset

"Divine pudding" **Sally Clarke**

"A very witty plate" **Alan Yentob**

RAVIOLI 'LAS VEGAS'

White Pasta:
125 g (4 oz) durum wheat flour
125 g (4 oz) plain flour
4 egg yolks
pinch of salt
15 ml (1 tbsp) olive oil
15 ml (1 tbsp) water

Black Pasta:
125 g (4 oz) durum wheat flour
125 g (4 oz) plain flour
2 sachets of black squid ink
3 egg yolks
pinch of salt
15 ml (1 tbsp) olive oil
15 ml (1 tbsp) water

Ravioli Filling:
30 ml (2 tbsp) olive oil
2 sticks celery, finely diced
15 ml (1 tbsp) finely chopped celery leaves
5 ml (1 tsp) finely grated fresh root ginger
10 ml (2 tsp) sesame seeds
225 g (8 oz) scallops, cleaned

Sauce:
175 ml (6 fl oz) double cream
1 lemon grass stalk, bruised
2 lime leaves
60 ml (4 tbsp) coconut milk
few drops of chilli oil
salt and freshly ground black pepper

To Garnish:
about 5 large scallops, cleaned
juice of 1 lime
5 ml (1 tsp) caviar eggs

To make the white pasta, put all of the ingredients in a food processor and work to a smooth, shiny, elastic dough. Wrap in cling film. Repeat with the ingredients for the black pasta. Leave both pastas to rest for at least 1 hour.

Meanwhile make the sauce. Put the ingredients in a saucepan over a low heat. Allow to simmer for 5 minutes, then remove from the heat and leave to infuse for 30 minutes.

For the garnish, cut the scallops into about twenty 1.5 cm (¾ inch) cubes. Sprinkle with the lime juice and leave to marinate for 30 minutes.

To make the ravioli filling, heat the oil in a pan and sauté the celery, celery leaves, ginger and sesame seeds until slightly golden. Allow to cool. Put three quarters of the scallops in a food processer with the cooled mixture and process for a few seconds until smooth. Finely dice the remaining scallops and stir into the puréed mixture. Season well.

To shape the ravioli, take one quarter of the white pasta and pass through the pasta machine on the no. 1 setting. Fold in half and pass through the machine a second time. Repeat with a quarter of the black pasta. Cut strips from these pieces, 15 cm (6 inches) long and 1 cm (½ inch) wide. Lay 8 strips side by side, alternating black and white pasta. Push these together firmly and pass through the machine repeatedly, narrowing the setting each time until the pasta is very thin.

Lay the striped pasta sheet on a tea-towel sprinkled lightly with durum wheat flour. Brush with water to dampen and place 3-4 mounds of filling along the length. Lay another striped pasta sheet over the top and press around each mound to seal firmly. Cut around the shaped ravioli, using a 7.5 cm (3 inch) fluted round cutter. Place these on another clean tea-towel sprinkled with flour. Repeat to make 12-16 ravioli.

Cook the ravioli in boiling salted water for 2 minutes. Meanwhile, strain the sauce and heat through. Pat the scallop garnish dry. Drain the cooked ravioli thoroughly. Pool the sauce on each warmed serving plate and place 3 or 4 raviolis on top. Put 5 scallop dice in the middle and dot caviar eggs on each one to resemble dice! Serve at once.

PIGEON BREASTS STUFFED WITH SMOKED AUBERGINE AND PICKLED WALNUTS

Use the pigeon carcasses to make a well-flavoured game stock for the sauce; prepare this well in advance. To smoke the aubergine, you will need a smoking box. As an alternative you could roast it.

4 pigeons' breasts
a little olive oil, for frying

Sauce:
250 ml (8 fl oz) well-flavoured game stock
   (see below)
2 bulbs of garlic, unpeeled but split
about 120 ml (4 fl oz) milk
15 ml (1 tbsp) olive oil
5 ml (1 tsp) sugar
175 ml (6 fl oz) double cream

Stuffing:
1 aubergine, halved lengthways
30 ml (2 tbsp) olive oil
2 pickled walnuts, chopped

Crispy Celery:
10 sticks celery
olive oil, for deep-frying

First make the sauce. Put the garlic in a pan, add sufficient milk to cover and simmer for 1 minute, then drain and coat with the oil and sugar. Roast in a preheated oven at 200°C (400°F) mark 6 for about 20 minutes until golden brown. Allow to cool, then peel and chop roughly. Put into a saucepan with the game stock and cream. Simmer for 10 minutes, then sieve into a clean pan, pressing through the garlic. Adjust the seasoning and keep warm.

Smoke the aubergine for 30 minutes, then allow to cool. Peel and chop the aubergine flesh. Heat the olive oil in a pan, add the aubergine with the pickled walnuts, and fry for 10 minutes. Allow to cool slightly, then process in a blender or food processor until smooth and check the seasoning.

Skin the pigeon breasts and make an incision into the middle of each one along its length. Stuff with the aubergine mixture. To cook, heat a little olive oil in a heavy-based pan. When very hot, add the pigeon breasts and sear on both sides. Roast in the oven at 200°C (400°F) mark 6 for 3 minutes, then cover with foil and leave to rest in a warm place while preparing the celery.

Remove the strings from the celery, then using a potato peeler, shave long thin 'noodles'. Dry the celery noodles very thoroughly with kitchen paper. Deep-fry in very hot olive oil, a few at a time, until they are golden and stop sizzling. Drain on kitchen paper; keep warm.

To serve, carve the pigeon breasts into thin slices. Pool the sauce onto warmed serving plates and put a small mound of cabbage in the middle. Cover with the pigeon slices. Form the celery into nests and place three on each plate around the pigeon. Spoon a heap of mashed turnip into each nest and top with the crispy shallots (see page 134). Put a small amount of celery on top of the pigeon. Serve at once.

Game Stock: Heat 15 ml (1 tbsp) oil in a large heavy-based pan and fry ½ finely chopped onion, 2 chopped celery sticks and 900 g (2 lb) chicken bones until dark brown. Add 2 chopped tomatoes, stirring to deglaze the pan. Add the pigeon carcasses and sufficient water to cover. Add a small bunch of strong herbs, such as bay, thyme and rosemary. Bring to the boil, lower the heat and simmer for several hours. Strain and allow to cool, then skim off the fat. Pass through a muslin-lined sieve into a clean pan and simmer to reduce to 250 ml (8 fl oz).

BRAISED RED CABBAGE

30 ml (2 tbsp) olive oil
1 onion, very finely shredded
15 ml (1 tbsp) sugar
1 large apple, peeled, cored and sliced
½ red cabbage, very finely shredded
2 bay leaves
15 ml (1 tbsp) sherry vinegar
4 juniper berries
60 ml (2 fl oz) water
salt and freshly ground black pepper

Heat the olive oil in a large heavy based pan. Add the onion and sauté until golden brown. Add the sugar and apple slices and cook, stirring frequently, until a rich caramel colour is obtained and the apple slices are fluffy. Stir in the red cabbage, bay leaves, vinegar, juniper berries and water. Season well. Cover with a tight-fitting lid and cook at a gentle simmer for about 1 hour, or until the cabbage is tender.

MASHED TURNIPS WITH CRISPY SHALLOTS

700 g (1½ lb) turnips, peeled and diced
50 g (2 oz) butter, plus 15 ml (1 tbsp)
6 large shallots, thinly sliced
150 ml (¼ pint) double cream
pinch of freshly grated nutmeg
salt and freshly ground black pepper
15 ml (1 tbsp) finely chopped parsley

Cook the turnips in a pan of simmering water for about 10 minutes until tender. Drain and purée in a food processor.

Melt 50 g (2 oz) butter in a heavy-based pan and gently sauté the shallots until golden brown and crisp; this may take at least 15 minutes. Drain on kitchen paper and keep warm.

Put the cream and 15 ml (1 tbsp) butter in a saucepan and bring to the boil. Add the turnips and stir briskly. Season generously with the nutmeg, salt and pepper, then stir in the chopped parsley. Serve immediately, topped with the crispy shallots.

CARAMELISED RASPBERRIES WITH A LEMON POSSET

Lemon Posset:
600 ml (1 pint) double cream
50 g (2 oz) sugar
finely grated rind and juice of 2 lemons
24 raspberries

Caramelised Raspberries:
250 g (9 oz) sugar
90 ml (6 tbsp) water
20 raspberries

To Decorate:
redcurrant sprigs or fresh raspberries

Put the cream, sugar and grated lemon rind in a saucepan and slowly bring to the boil. Meanwhile pour the lemon juice into a large bowl. Pour the hot cream mixture onto the lemon juice, stirring gently to mix. Cool quickly over crushed ice or in the refrigerator.

Line 4 ramekins with cling film and arrange 6 raspberries in the base of each one. Pour on just enough of the lemon mixture to cover them. Chill in the refrigerator for 15 minutes. Pour on the rest of the lemon mixture and refrigerate for at least 2 hours, or preferably overnight.

For the caramelised raspberries, dissolve the sugar in the water in a heavy-based saucepan over a low heat. Increase the heat and boil rapidly to a golden caramel. Remove from the heat. One at a time, spear the raspberries on a skewer and dip into the caramel, turning to coat. Transfer to a tray lined with non-stick baking parchment and leave to cool.

To serve, turn the puddings out onto individual serving plates. Surround with the caramelised raspberries and redcurrant sprigs or fresh raspberries.

SEMI-FINAL

GERRY GOLDWYRE • ANDREA FERRARI • CONNIE STEVENS

PANEL OF JUDGES

Robert Carrier • Sue Lawley • Loyd Grossman

WINNER

GERRY GOLDWYRE'S MENU

STARTER

*Roast Kyle of Lochalsh Prawns
with Crispy Carrot and Courgette Topping*

MAIN COURSE

*Pan-fried Border Wood Pigeon Breasts
with Wild Mushroom Sauce served on a bed of Puy Lentils
with Morel Mushrooms and a Celeriac Topping*

"The lentils were marvelous" **Robert Carrier**

DESSERT

*Banana Parfait
with Caramelised Bananas and Chocolate Sauce*

"Gosh – I loved it" **Robert Carrier**

ROAST KYLE OF LOCHALSH PRAWNS WITH CRISPY CARROT AND COURGETTE TOPPING

If possible, leave the prawns to marinate for 24 hours before cooking.

20 large raw prawns
vegetable oil for deep-frying
maldon salt
freshly ground white pepper
squeeze of lemon juice
5 ml (1 tsp) sunflower oil
dash of soy sauce

Marinade:
30 ml (2 tbsp) chilli oil
finely pared rind and juice of 1 lemon
1 clove garlic
1 small red chilli, deseeded and cut into thin
   strips
45 ml (3 tbsp) vegetable oil
2 cm (¾ inch) piece pickled or fresh root
   ginger, shredded
20-25 coriander leaves, roughly chopped

Topping:
1 carrot
2 courgettes

To Garnish:
chopped coriander leaves
a little finely chopped red pepper

Remove the heads from the prawns. Split them in half lengthwise and remove the black intestinal thread. Lay the prawns in a shallow dish. Mix together the ingredients for the marinade and spread evenly over the prawns. Cover the dish with cling film and leave to marinate in the refrigerator for at least 2 hours.

To prepare the topping, cut the carrot and courgettes into fine julienne strips and pat dry with kitchen paper. Heat the oil for deep-frying in a wok or deep-fat fryer to 190°C (375°F), or until a cube of bread dropped in turns golden brown in 40 seconds. Add the carrot and courgette strips and deep-fry for approximately 1 minute until crisp and golden brown. Drain on kitchen paper, season with salt and keep hot.

Heat some fresh oil for deep-frying in the wok or deep-fryer, as before. Remove the prawns from the marinade, using a slotted metal spoon, and add to the hot oil. Take care, as the oil is likely to splutter. Toss the prawns in the oil for 20-30 seconds until the shells are browned. Drain on kitchen paper, then season with salt and pepper and sprinkle with a little lemon juice.

Arrange the prawns in a circle on each warmed serving plate. Drizzle 5 ml (1 tsp) sunflower oil around them and dot with tiny drops of soy sauce. Pile the crisp-fried vegetables in the middle. Serve at once, garnished with coriander leaves and red pepper.

PAN-FRIED WOOD PIGEON BREASTS WITH WILD MUSHROOM SAUCE

Ask your butcher for the pigeon carcasses –
to make a well-flavoured stock for the sauce.

8 pigeon breasts
40 g (1½ oz) lentils de Puy
10 cloves garlic
3 bay leaves
3 thyme sprigs
maldon salt
freshly ground white pepper
65 g (2½ oz) unsalted butter
10 shallots, chopped
25 g (1 oz) button mushrooms, sliced
200 ml (7 fl oz) good red wine
300 ml (½ pint) strong pigeon stock
75 g (3 oz) piece celeriac
vegetable oil for deep-frying
15 ml (1 tbsp) duck fat or lard
squeeze of lemon juice
50 g (2 oz) morels or other wild mushrooms,
    cleaned
75 g (3 oz) smoked streaky bacon, derinded
    and cut into strips
15 ml (1 tbsp) double cream
15 ml (1 tbsp) chopped tarragon

Soak the lentils in cold water to cover
for at least 2 hours, or overnight if possible. Drain, place in a saucepan and
cover with clean water. Add 3 garlic
cloves, 2 bay leaves, 1 thyme sprig and
salt, then bring to the boil. Lower the
heat and cook for about 12-15 minutes
until the lentils are just softened (not
split). Drain, discarding the thyme,
garlic and bay leaves. Adjust the seasoning and set aside in a warm place.

Meanwhile, prepare the sauce. Melt
40 g (1½ oz) butter in a pan. Chop the
remaining garlic and add to the pan
with the shallots, thyme sprig, bay leaf
and button mushrooms. Cook until softened and beginning to caramelise. Add
the wine and simmer until it has almost

completely evaporated. Add the stock
and reduce by half. Strain the sauce,
then reheat and check the seasoning.

Thinly slice the celeriac, using a
mandolin if possible. Heat the oil in a
deep-fat fryer to 190°C (375°F). Test by
dropping in a slice of celeriac - if it
bubbles to the surface the oil is ready.
Slowly add the celeriac to the hot oil and
cook until crisp and golden brown.
Drain on kitchen paper; keep hot.

To cook the pigeon breasts, place a
large heavy-based frying pan over a
high heat. When it is very hot, add the
duck fat. Once the fat is smoking, add
the duck breasts to the pan, one at a
time. Cook for 20-30 seconds each side
until they start to change colour.
Transfer to a preheated oven at 230°C
(450°F) mark 8, adding a knob of butter
and a squeeze of lemon juice. Cook for 1
minute, then cover and leave to rest in a
warm place for 15-20 minutes.

To cook the wild mushrooms, place
the clean frying pan over a high heat.
Add 15 g (½ oz) butter and, when it has
melted, add the mushrooms and seasoning. Cook over a high heat for 2 minutes
or until the mushrooms change colour.
Drain, then return to the pan and toss
over the heat for another 20 seconds.
Season with salt and pepper to taste,
then add to the sauce.

Just before serving, dry-fry the bacon
in a small frying pan until crisp. Add a
small knob of butter, the juice from the
pigeon breasts (after resting), and the
lentils; stir well. Reheat the sauce and
stir in the cream and tarragon.

To serve, divide the lentils between
warmed serving plates. Split each
pigeon breast diagonally to form a
wedge, then lay on top of the lentils to
form a circle. Arrange the mushrooms
evenly around and pour the sauce over
them. Top the pigeon breasts with the
celeriac curls and serve at once.

Banana Parfait with Caramelised Bananas and Chocolate Sauce

Parfait:
6 egg yolks
125 g (4 oz) icing sugar
7.5 ml (1½ tsp) boiling water
300 ml (½ pint) double cream
3 ripe bananas
juice of 1 lemon

Caramelised Bananas:
2 bananas
lemon juice, for sprinkling
15 g (½ oz) icing sugar

Chocolate Sauce:
75 g (3 oz) quality plain chocolate, in pieces
120 ml (4 fl oz) milk (approximately)
15 ml (1 tbsp) dark rum

To prepare the parfait, whisk the egg yolks, icing sugar and boiling water together in a bowl until thick and fluffy. In another bowl, whip the cream until it begins to stiffen.

Peel the bananas and place in a blender or food processor with the lemon juice. Process until smooth. Fold the banana purée into the whisked egg yolk mixture, then fold in the whipped cream. Divide the parfait mixture between individual moulds, cover and place in the freezer for 2-3 hours until set firm.

To prepare the caramelised bananas, peel and cut into thick slices on the diagonal. Sprinkle with lemon juice and dredge with icing sugar. Place under a preheated very hot grill until caramelised, turning once. Set aside to cool.

To make the chocolate sauce, melt the chocolate with the milk in a heatproof bowl over a pan of hot water. Stir until evenly blended. The sauce should have a smooth pouring consistency; if necessary thin with a little more milk. Stir in the rum.

To serve, unmould the parfaits onto individual serving plates and surround with the caramelised banana slices. Pour the chocolate sauce over the parfaits and serve at once.

THE SECOND
SEMI-FINAL
GERRY GOLDWYRE • ANDREA FERRARI • CONNIE STEVENS

PANEL OF JUDGES
Robert Carrier • Sue Lawley • Loyd Grossman

ANDREA FERRARI'S MENU

STARTER

Tataki of Tuna
with Pickled Vegetables

"Fantastically interesting" **Robert Carrier**

MAIN COURSE

Fillet of Spiced Venison
with Mulled Fruits

Grilled Polenta

Steamed Mangetouts

"I went mad for the grilled polenta" **Robert Carrier**

DESSERT

Walnut Tartlets
with Crème Fraîche

"Perfect" **Robert Carrier**

TATAKI OF TUNA WITH PICKLED VEGETABLES

This recipe is an adaptation of one from Anton Mossiman.

175 g (6 oz) very fresh tuna fillet, in one piece
salt and freshly ground black pepper
small bunch of coriander
small bunch of flat-leaved parsley
small bunch of basil
30 ml (2 tbsp) English mustard
30 ml (2 tbsp) very finely chopped fresh root ginger
30 ml (2 tbsp) finely chopped garlic

To Serve:
pickled peppers or other vegetables (preferably homemade)

Season the tuna with salt and pepper. Place a heavy-based frying pan over a high heat. Add the tuna and sear (without oil) for about 1 minute on each side. The fish should be sealed and lightly cooked at the edges, but still pink in the middle.

Finely chop the herbs and mix with the mustard, ginger and garlic. Roll the tuna in the herb mixture to liberally coat all four sides. Wrap in cling film and refrigerate until ready to serve.

Immediately prior to serving, slice the tuna very thinly, dress with the herb mixture and accompany with pickled vegetables.

FILLET OF SPICED VENISON WITH MULLED FRUITS

For this recipe, you really need to marinate the venison and fruits 24 hours ahead.

4 venison fillets, trimmed
16 dried figs or prunes
16 dried apricots
600 ml (1 pint) red wine
2 sachets of mulling spices, or 3 cinnamon sticks, 8 crushed juniper berries and 12 cloves
15 ml (1 tbsp) olive oil
salt and freshly ground black pepper

Lay the venison fillets in a shallow dish with the dried fruits. Pour in the wine and add the spices. Cover and leave to marinate for 24 hours.

Lift the venison fillets out of the marinade. Remove and discard the spices from the marinade. Heat the olive oil in a frying pan, add the venison fillets and cook for about 3 minutes each side, depending on the thickness of the meat. Ideally it should still be quite pink inside. Remove the meat from the pan; cover and keep warm.

Add the marinade and fruit to the pan, stirring to scrape up the sediment. Allow the sauce to simmer, uncovered, for about 15 minutes, until reduced by half and slightly thickened. Season with salt and pepper to taste.

Cut each venison fillet into 6 slices and return to the pan. Heat through for 1-2 minutes, then arrange the venison slices in a fan-shape on each warmed serving plate. Surround with the mulled fruits and sauce. Serve at once, accompanied by the grilled polenta and steamed mangetouts.

GRILLED POLENTA

175 g (6 oz) polenta flour
salt
freshly grated Parmesan cheese

Bring 1.2 litres (2 pints) of salted water to the boil in a heavy-based saucepan. Add the polenta flour and stir vigorously for 5 minutes, to ensure that no lumps form.

Pour the polenta into a lightly buttered shallow baking tin, to a depth of about 2 cm (¾ inch). Allow to cool and solidify.

Using a 5-7.5 cm (2-3 inch) pastry cutter, cut out circles of polenta allowing 2-3 per person. Sprinkle with grated Parmesan cheese and flash under a preheated hot grill until the cheese has melted and the polenta is heated through. Serve at once.

WALNUT TARTLETS WITH CRÈME FRAÎCHE

Flan Pastry:
75 g (3 oz) plain flour
65 g (2½ oz) butter, diced
40 g (1½ oz) icing sugar, sifted
2 egg yolks
1 drop of vanilla essence

Walnut Filling:
125 g (4 oz) shelled walnuts
50 g (2 oz) butter
75 g (3 oz) caster sugar
10 ml (2 tsp) honey
10 ml (2 tsp) liquid glucose
125 ml (4 fl oz) double cream
25 g (1 oz) sultanas, soaked in a little
  rum or liqueur to taste

To Serve:
icing sugar, for dusting
créme fraîche

To make the pastry, sift the flour onto a work surface. Make a well in the centre and add the butter, icing sugar, egg yolks and vanilla essence. Using the fingertips of one hand, mix the ingredients in the well together, then gradually work in the flour to bind the dough. Knead lightly until smooth, then wrap in cling film and chill in the refrigerator for 30 minutes.

Roll out the chilled dough to a thickness of 3 mm (⅛ inch). Cut out 4 rounds and use to line 10 cm (4 inch) individual tartlet tins. Leave to rest in the refrigerator for 20 minutes. Line the tartlet cases with greaseproof paper and baking beans and bake blind in a preheated oven at 200°C (400°F) mark 6 for 10 minutes. Remove the paper and beans and return to the oven for about 5 minutes to cook the bases. Allow to cool, then remove from the tins.

Spread the walnuts on a baking tray and place in a preheated oven at 120°C (250°F) mark ½ for 10 minutes. Meanwhile, place the butter, sugar, honey and glucose in a heavy-based pan over a very low heat until melted, stirring continuously. Continue to heat the mixture until it becomes caramel-coloured. Remove from the heat and carefully stir in the cream. Return briefly to the heat and allow to bubble for a further 1 minute. Add the walnuts and sultanas.

Divide the walnut mixture between the pastry cases and leave to stand at room temperature for 1 hour before serving. Dust with icing sugar to serve and accompany with crème fraîche.

SEMI-FINAL
GERRY GOLDWYRE • ANDREA FERRARI • CONNIE STEVENS

PANEL OF JUDGES
Robert Carrier • Sue Lawley • Loyd Grossman

CONNIE STEVENS' MENU

STARTER
*Mousseline of Lemon Sole and Asparagus
with 'Fish Toasties'*

MAIN COURSE
*Fillet of Beef filled with Oriental Mushrooms
Creamed Potatoes with Sweet Red Peppers and Leek
French Beans sautéed in Butter and Ginger*

DESSERT
*Blueberry and Cream Tartlet
on a Mixed Berry Sauce*

"Smashing" **Sue Lawley**

MOUSSELINE OF LEMON SOLE AND ASPARAGUS WITH 'FISH TOASTIES'

Chill the two mixing bowls needed for this recipe in the refrigerator for half an hour before using them.

8 thin asparagus spears
175 g (6 oz) skinned and filleted lemon sole
1 egg white (size 2)
salt
75 ml (2½ fl oz) crème fraîche
450 ml (¾ pint) double cream
cayenne pepper, to taste
15 g (½ oz) butter, melted

To Serve:
4 slices of wholemeal bread
few blanched and sautéed asparagus tips,
* or salad leaves, to garnish*

Blanch the asparagus spears in warm water for 1 minute. Drain and dry well with kitchen paper. Place the asparagus in a blender or food processor and purée for 30 seconds. Set aside.

Check the lemon sole is free of skin and bones; remove any fine bones with a tweezer. Purée the sole in a blender, then transfer to a bowl, set over a larger bowl filled with crushed ice. Add the egg white and a generous pinch of salt and beat thoroughly until the mixture becomes firm and tight. Gradually beat in the crème fraîche until evenly blended, then repeat with the double cream. Mix in the puréed asparagus. Season with cayenne pepper to taste.

Brush 4 ramekins with melted butter. Fill with the sole and asparagus mixture, leaving 5 mm (¼ inch) at the top to allow for some expansion during cooking. Cover with buttered foil. Place the ramekins in a steamer and steam lightly for 20 minutes.

Whilst the mousselines are steaming, prepare the fish toasties. Cut 4 fish shapes out of each slice of bread and toast until crisp and browned on both sides. Keep warm until ready to serve.

Turn the mousselines out onto individual serving plates and garnish with asparagus or salad leaves. Serve at once, accompanied by the 'fish toasties'.

Note: The mousselines can be kept warm in the steamer (with the heat off) for up to 15 minutes prior to serving.

Roquefort and Spring Onion Tartlets
FIONA PHELPS' STARTER (Semi-Final)

Medallions of Skye Monkfish with Trompet and Tarragon Sauce
GERRY GOLDWYRE'S MAIN COURSE (Final)

FILLET OF BEEF WITH ORIENTAL MUSHROOMS

575 g (1½ lb) fillet of beef, in one piece
15 g (½ oz) dried wild ceps or porcini
40 g (1½ oz) butter
225 g (8 oz) mixed fresh mushrooms
  (eg shiitake, oyster and brown cap)
2 cloves garlic, crushed
30 ml (2 tbsp) rich soy sauce
7.5 ml (1½ tsp) sweet chilli sauce
45 ml (3 tbsp) black bean sauce
10 ml (2 tsp) yellow bean sauce
10 ml (2 tsp) oyster sauce
5 ml (1 tsp) five-spice powder
salt and freshly ground black pepper
2.5-5 ml (½ -1 tsp) sugar

Put the dried mushrooms in a bowl, pour on 175 ml (6 fl oz) hot water and leave to soak for 20 minutes.

Melt 25 g (1 oz) of the butter in a pan, add the fresh mushrooms and garlic and cook over a medium heat for 3-4 minutes. Drain the soaked mushrooms, reserving the liquid, add to the pan and cook for 2 minutes. Stir in the oriental sauces, then add the five-spice powder and cook for a further 1 minute. Season with salt and pepper, and add sugar to taste. Add the reserved mushroom soaking liquid and cook over a medium heat until the sauce is reduced and thickened. Add 175 ml (6 fl oz) water and reduce once more, until thickened.

Insert a long pointed knife into one end of the beef fillet to make a slit through to the centre. Repeat from the other end – hopefully meeting in the middle – to form a cavity for the stuffing. With a slotted spoon, remove some of the mushrooms from the sauce and use to fill the beef fillet cavity. Either sew up both ends or secure with skewers.

Melt the remaining butter and brush over the stuffed beef fillet. Place under a preheated medium grill for 7 minutes, turning occasionally to seal on all sides. Transfer to a baking tray and cook in a preheated oven at 180°C (350°F) mark 4 for 20 minutes for rare meat, or longer if preferred.

When cooked, cover the beef and leave to stand in a warm place for 5 minutes. Meanwhile, reheat the mushroom sauce. Cut the beef into thick slices and place on warmed serving plates. Pour the mushrooms and sauce over and around the beef. Serve at once, with the accompaniments.

CREAMED POTATOES WITH SWEET RED PEPPERS AND LEEK

900 g (2 lb) potatoes (eg Belle de Fontenay
  or King Edward)
50 g (2 oz) butter
2 shallots, finely chopped
4 medium leeks, trimmed and finely sliced
5 baby sweet red peppers, deseeded and
  finely sliced
1 egg yolk
60 ml (4 tbsp) crème fraîche
salt and freshly ground black pepper

Cut the potatoes into even-sized pieces and cook in boiling water until just tender. Drain and peel when cool enough to handle. Meanwhile, melt 25 g (1 oz) of the butter in a pan, add the shallots, leeks and red peppers and sauté lightly until cooked, but still retaining a bite.

Mash the cooked potatoes thoroughly with the remaining butter and egg yolk. Add the sautéed pepper, leeks and shallot mixture and stir well. Season with salt and pepper to taste. Serve immediately.

Note: If baby sweet peppers are unobtainable, use 2 or 3 regular ones instead. Note that potatoes are best cooked in their skins, then peeled after cooking.

FRENCH BEANS SAUTÉED IN BUTTER AND GINGER

225 g (8 oz) French beans, trimmed
40 g (1½ oz) butter
15 g (½ oz) caster sugar
25 g (1 oz) fresh root ginger, peeled and
  grated or crushed
salt and freshly ground black pepper

Cook the French beans in boiling water to cover for 5 minutes. Drain and refresh with cold water, then drain again. Set aside until ready to serve.

Melt the butter in a small pan. Add the cooked beans, sugar and ginger and heat through, stirring, for 2 minutes. Season with salt and pepper to taste. Serve immediately.

BLUEBERRY AND CREAM TARTLET ON A MIXED BERRY SAUCE

The quantities given below for the pastry are sufficient for 6 tartlets. Freeze the remainder, or store in the refrigerator for 2-3 days.

Pastry:
225 g (8 oz) plain flour
125 g (4 oz) icing sugar
125 g (4 oz) butter, softened
1 egg (size 2)
white vegetable fat, for greasing

Filling:
350 g (12 oz) blueberries
3 egg yolks
75 g (3 oz) caster sugar
60 ml (4 tbsp) crème fraîche
150 ml (¼ pint) double cream

Sauce:
handful of blueberries
*300 g (10 oz) can blackberries in natural
   juice, plus the juice from a second can*
15 ml (5 tbsp) gin (preferably Plymouth gin)
45 ml (3 tbsp) caster sugar

To Decorate:
*15 ml (1 tbsp) crème fraîche, warmed to
   thin consistency*

Place all of the ingredients for the pastry in a food processor and process until smooth. Wrap in cling film and chill in the refrigerator for at least 30 minutes. Meanwhile grease four 10 cm (4 inch) individual tartlet tins with a little white vegetable fat. Roll out the pastry to a 2 mm (¹⁄₁₀ inch) thickness and use to line the tartlet tins.

Arrange a layer of blueberries in the base of each pastry case. Whisk the egg yolks with the caster sugar. Add the crème fraîche, then beat in the double cream. Spoon the mixture over the blueberries in the tartlet cases. Bake in a preheated oven at 190°C (375°F) mark 5 for 5 minutes, then lower the temperature to 160°C (325°F) mark 3 and bake for a further 10-12 minutes. Leave in the tins for 10 minutes, then turn out.

Meanwhile, prepare the sauce. Put the blueberries into a small pan. Add the blackberries with their juice and the sugar. Bring to the boil and reduce until syrupy. Add the gin and heat for a further 30 seconds.

Place a tartlet in the centre of each serving plate. Spoon some of the warm berry sauce around each tartlet, decorate with droplets of crème fraîche and feather with a skewer. Serve at once.

SEMI-FINAL

ALISON FIANDER • ROGER HEMMING • FIONA PHELPS

PANEL OF JUDGES

Michel Bourdin • Egon Ronay • Loyd Grossman

WINNER

ALISON FIANDER'S MENU

STARTER

Salmon Naan with Pesto and Balsamico Cream

MAIN COURSE

Macadamia and Sesame Chicken on Thai-style Salad

"The flavour of the chicken was outstanding" **Egon Ronay**

DESSERT

Cappucino Cup

"The taste was excellent" **Michel Bourdin**

SALMON NAAN WITH PESTO AND BALSAMIEO CREAM

4 naan breads
250 g (9 oz) smoked salmon, thinly sliced
freshly ground black pepper

Pesto:
about 50 g (2 oz) basil leaves
1 clove garlic, peeled
scant 25 g (1 oz) pine nuts
scant 25 g (1 oz) freshly grated Parmesan cheese
60 ml (2 fl oz) virgin olive oil (approximately)
salt and freshly ground black pepper

Balsamico Cream:
90 ml (3 fl oz) soured cream
60 ml (2 fl oz) natural yogurt
5-10 ml (1-2 tsp) balsamic vinegar
7.5 ml (1½ tsp) chopped chives
7.5 ml (1½ tsp) chopped basil

To Garnish:
basil sprigs

To make the pesto, put the basil leaves in a food processor and process until finely chopped. Add the garlic, pine nuts and Parmesan and process until well combined. With the motor still running, slowly pour in the olive oil through the feeder tube, until the pesto is the desired consistency. Transfer to a bowl and season with salt and pepper to taste. Set aside.

To make the balsamico cream, mix together all the ingredients in a bowl, cover and refrigerate until ready to serve.

To assemble and serve, heat the naan bread in a preheated oven at 200°C (400°F) mark 6 for a few minutes until warm and slightly crisp. Place on warmed serving plates and spread each naan with some balsamico cream. Top with slices of smoked salmon and drizzle over some of the pesto. Sprinkle with pepper, garnish with basil and serve immediately.

MACADAMIA AND SESAME CHICKEN

500 g (1 lb) chicken fillets
30 ml (2 tbsp) light soy sauce
125 g (4 oz) macadamia nuts, finely chopped
75 ml (5 tbsp) sesame seeds
1 egg white
salt
30 ml (2 tbsp) cornflour
peanut oil, for shallow-frying

To Serve:
Thai-style salad (see right)
red chillies, to garnish
soy sauce flavoured with chilli slices, for
dipping

Cut the chicken into thin slices and place in a shallow dish. Add the soy sauce, turn to coat and leave to marinate for 1 hour.

Combine the chopped nuts and sesame seeds in a flat dish. Beat the egg white with a pinch of salt until light and frothy. Dip the chicken pieces into the cornflour, then in the egg white. Finally coat with the nut mixture, pressing it on firmly.

Heat the oil for shallow-frying in a frying pan until a heat haze rises. Shallow-fry the chicken in batches until golden brown. Drain well on kitchen paper and keep warm while cooking the remainder.

To serve, divide the salad between serving plates and top with the warm chicken. Garnish with chillies and serve at once, with the dipping sauce.

THAI-STYLE SALAD

125 g (4 oz) sugar snap peas
125 g (4 oz) baby sweetcorn, halved
lengthways
¼ Chinese cabbage
½ red pepper, cored and deseeded
½ bunch spring onions, trimmed
2 carrots, peeled
¼ fresh pineapple, peeled and cored
125 g (4 oz) oyster mushrooms
handful (¼ cup) coriander leaves, roughly
torn

Dressing:
45 ml (3 tbsp) groundnut oil
45 ml (3 tbsp) rice wine vinegar
5 ml (1 tsp) wasabi paste
5 ml (1 tsp) sugar
salt and freshly ground black pepper

Blanch the sugar snap peas and baby sweetcorn separately in boiling water for 1 minute. Drain and refresh under cold water; drain thoroughly. Finely shred the cabbage; finely slice the red pepper. Cut the spring onions into thin strips, on the diagonal. Pare the carrots into thin strips, using a vegetable peeler. Cut the fresh pineapple into finger-sized sticks. Combine these salad ingredients in a bowl.

Sauté the oyster mushrooms briefly in the groundnut oil for the dressing. Remove with a slotted spoon and add to the salad. Add the rest of the ingredients for the dressing to the pan and stir well. Pour over the salad, add the coriander leaves and toss well to serve.

CAPPUCINO CUP

30 ml (2 tbsp) cold black coffee
10 ml (2 tsp) gelatine
3 eggs (size 2), separated
75 g (3 oz) caster sugar
15 ml (1 tbsp) brandy (optional)
300 ml (½ pint) double cream
grated plain chocolate, to decorate

Put the cold black coffee in a small bowl, sprinkle on the gelatine and leave to soften. Place the bowl over a pan of simmering water until the gelatine is dissolved. Allow to cool.

Whisk the egg yolks and caster sugar together in a bowl for 5 minutes or until pale and thick. Add the brandy if desired. In another bowl whip 150 ml (¼ pint) of the cream until it forms soft peaks.

In a separate bowl, whisk the egg whites until they form soft peaks.

Stir the dissolved gelatine and coffee mixture into the whisked eggs and sugar, then fold in the whipped cream. Finally fold in the whisked egg whites. Place in the refrigerator to set.

To serve, spoon the mousse into serving cups. Whip the remaining cream and spread on top of the mousses. Sprinkle with grated chocolate to decorate.

PANEL OF JUDGES
Michel Bourdin • Egon Ronay • Loyd Grossman

ROGER HEMMING'S MENU

STARTER
Warm Salad of Scallops scented with Cumin

MAIN COURSE
*Pan-fried Breast of Wood Pigeon with
a Wild Rowanberry Sauce
Soufflé of Mashed Potato
Roasted Root Vegetables*

"The balance of flavour and texture was superb" **Michel Bourdin**

DESSERT
Pink Gin Syllabub with an Angostura Sauce
"An amazing experience" **Egon Ronay**

WARM SALAD OF SCALLOPS SCENTED WITH CUMIN

8 large scallops, with corals, cleaned
2 rashers smoked streaky bacon, derinded
and cut into strips
30 ml (2 tbsp) pine nuts
pinch of ground cumin
assorted salad leaves (eg corn salad, frisée,
lollo rosso, rocket)
squeeze of lemon juice

Vinaigrette:
15 ml (1 tbsp) white wine vinegar
1.25 ml (¼ tsp) sugar
1.25 ml (¼ tsp) dry English mustard
salt and freshly ground black pepper
7.5 ml (½ tbsp) hazelnut oil
45 ml (3 tbsp) corn oil

First make the vinaigrette. Mix the wine vinegar, sugar and mustard together in a bowl with a pinch of salt and a couple of twists of black pepper. Drizzle in the hazelnut and corn oils, whisking constantly to form an even emulsion.

Dry-fry the bacon strips in a heavy-based non-stick frying pan, without additional fat, until crispy. Remove with a slotted spoon and set aside; reserve the bacon fat in the pan, too.

Spread the pine nuts on a baking tray and toast under a hot grill until just starting to brown. Set aside.

Shortly before serving, prepare and cook the scallops. Remove the corals and set aside, then carefully cut the white meat horizontally in half, to provide two discs from each scallop. Place the non-stick frying pan (used for the bacon) over a moderate heat. When it is very hot, add the cumin, stir briefly with a wooden spoon, then add the scallop discs. Cook for no more than 30 to 40 seconds, then turn and cook the other side. Season with a little salt and pepper, then sprinkle with a squeeze of lemon juice. Remove from the heat. Briefly sauté the scallop corals in the same pan for 10-15 seconds.

To serve, toss the salad leaves in the vinaigrette and pile a mound in the centre of each serving plate. Surround with the white scallops and top with the reserved corals, pine nuts and bacon.

PAN-FRIED BREAST OF WOOD PIGEON WITH A WILD ROWANBERRY SAUCE

Use the pigeon carcasses to prepare a well-flavoured stock for the sauce, in advance. Ideally the pigeon breasts should be allowed to marinate overnight.

4 wood pigeons, plucked and drawn

Marinade:
¼ bottle full-bodied red wine
30 ml (2 tbsp) olive oil
1 clove garlic, crushed
2 bay leaves
1 thyme sprig or 5 ml (1 tsp) dried thyme
6 black peppercorns
salt and freshly ground black pepper

Sauce:
150 ml (¼ pint) well-flavoured pigeon stock (see below)
30 ml (2 tbsp) rowan jelly
½ square dark bitter chocolate
40 g (1½ oz) unsalted butter, in pieces

Croûtons:
4 slices wholemeal bread
25 g (1 oz) butter
15 ml (1 tbsp) hazelnut oil

To Garnish:
lamb's lettuce, dressed in a little vinaigrette
12 steamed sugar snap peas or mangetouts

Remove the breasts from the pigeons, using a sharp knife. Use the pigeon carcasses to make the stock (see below).

For the marinade, combine the red wine, olive oil, garlic, bay leaves, thyme, black peppercorns and a pinch of salt in a large bowl. Add the pigeon breasts, turn to coat and leave to marinate for at least 5 hours, preferably overnight.

Shortly before serving, prepare the croûtons. Using a mug or similar-sized guide, cut a disc from each slice of wholemeal bread. Melt the butter in a frying pan with the hazelnut oil. When hot, add the bread rounds and fry, turning once, until crisp and golden brown on both sides. Drain on kitchen paper and keep warm.

Lift the pigeon breasts out of the marinade and pat dry with kitchen paper. Strain the marinade and reserve. Place a non-stick frying pan over a moderate heat (without any fat). When it is very hot, add the pigeon breasts and sear for 2-3 minutes each side. Remove, cover with foil and leave to rest in a warm place.

Add the strained marinade to the pan, stirring with a wooden spoon to scrape up any sediment. Transfer to a saucepan and add the pigeon stock. Slowly bring to the boil, skim, then add the rowan jelly and stir until melted. Add the chocolate and again stir until incorporated. Simmer to reduce by one third or until the sauce has a syrupy consistency. Whisk in the butter, a piece at a time, and season with salt and pepper to taste.

To serve, slice each pigeon breast horizontally in two. Pool the sauce on the warmed serving plates and float a croûton in the centre. Arrange the pigeon slices on the croûton and top with a little lamb's lettuce. Garnish with sugar snap peas or mangetouts and serve with the accompaniments.

Pigeon Stock: Chop the pigeon carcasses, place in a roasting tin and roast in a preheated oven at 450°C (230°F) mark 8 for 30 minutes until well browned. Transfer to a large saucepan and add 1.2 litres (2 pints) water, 1 chopped onion, 1 chopped carrot, 1 chopped celery stick and a bouquet garni. Bring to the boil and simmer for 3-4 hours. Strain and use as required.

SOUFFLÉ OF MASHED POTATO

4 even-shaped medium new potatoes
4 medium old potatoes
salt and freshly ground black pepper
2 eggs, separated
knob of butter
15 ml (1 tbsp) double cream
5 ml (1 tsp) chopped herbs (thyme, chervil,
  parsley etc)
5 ml (1 tsp) melted duck fat, or lard
5 ml (1 tsp) coarse sea salt

Bake the new potatoes in their skins in a preheated oven at 200°C (400°F) mark 6 for 20-25 minutes until cooked. Allow to cool then, using a sharp knife, cut the top off each potato taking care not to break the sides. Carefully scoop out the inside flesh, using a melon baller, leaving a 3 mm (⅛ inch) shell. Discard the scooped-out potato flesh.

Boil the other potatoes in salted water until tender. Drain, mash and push through a fine sieve. Beat the egg white in a bowl until it holds its shape, then add 1 egg yolk. Fold a knob of butter and the double cream into the mashed potato, then fold in the herbs, beaten egg and seasoning.

Using a piping bag fitted with a plain nozzle, pipe the potato mixture into each of the four potato shells. Beat the remaining egg yolk and carefully brush over the surface of the potato soufflés. Brush the potato shells with a little melted duck fat. Sprinkle the soufflés with sea salt and bake in a preheated oven at 180°C (350°F) mark 4 for 12-15 minutes until just browned on the top. Serve immediately.

ROASTED ROOT VEGETABLES

2 large carrots
2 medium turniops
1 large sweet potato
2 medium beetroot
30 ml (2 tbsp) duck fat
salt and freshly ground black pepper

Peel the root vegetables, keeping the beetroot separate to prevent the colour bleeding. Using an apple corer, cut 4 even-sized cylinders from each vegetable. Put a tablespoonful of duck fat in each of two small roasting tins and place on the hob to melt the fat. Roll the turnip, sweet potato and carrot cylinders in one tin; roll the beetroot cylinders in the other one. Season with salt and pepper.

Transfer to a preheated oven at 200°C (400° F) mark 6 and bake, turning occasionally, for 20-25 minutes until browned. Serve at once.

PINK GIN SYLLABUB WITH AN ANGOSTURA SAUCE

Syllabub:
5 ml (1 tsp) freshly ground mixed spice
   (see note)
105 ml (7 tbsp) gin
grated rind and juice of 1 lemon
15 ml (1 tbsp) angostura bitters
50 g (2 oz) caster sugar
1 drop of red food colouring
300 ml (½ pint) double cream

Angostura Sauce:
grated rind and juice of 1 lemon
150 g (5 oz) caster sugar
45 ml (3 tbsp) angostura bitters
45 ml (3 tbsp) water

Candied Lemon Zest:
finely pared rind of 1 lemon
25 g (1 oz) caster sugar
15 ml (1 tbsp) warm water
10 ml (2 tsp) grenadine

To Decorate:
mint sprigs

To make the syllabub, put the ground spice, gin, lemon rind and juice, angostura bitters and sugar in a bowl. Stir until the sugar is dissolved, then cover and leave to stand for 20 minutes. Strain into a mixing bowl and add the red colouring. Whisk, using an electric beater, then slowly add the cream in a steady stream, whisking constantly. As soon as the cream starts to thicken stop whisking, otherwise it will separate. Cover and chill in the refrigerator.

Meanwhile prepare the candied lemon zest. Cut the finely pared lemon rind into fine shreds, using a sharp knife. Blanch briefly in boiling water and drain. Dissolve the sugar in the water in a small pan over a low heat, then add the grenadine and bring to the boil. Add the lemon zest shreds and simmer for 10-15 minutes until candied. Remove the pink zests with a slotted spoon and spread out on a plate to cool.

To make the angostura sauce, put the lemon rind and juice in a a saucepan with the sugar, water and angostura bitters. Place over a low heat until the sugar is dissolved, then bring to the boil and cook gently until you have a blush pink syrup with an aromatic lemon flavour. Strain and check the consistency: the sauce should just coat the back of a spoon; if too thick, add a drop or two of hot water.

To serve, pool a thin layer of the angostura sauce on each serving plate. Using two spoons dipped in hot water, quickly shape the syllabub into quenelles and arrange three on each plate, radiating from the centre. Decorate with the candied zests and mint sprigs. Serve immediately.

Note: For the mixed spice, grind 1 clove, 1 allspice berry, a 2.5 cm (1 inch) piece of cinnamon stick and 1 juniper berry with a pinch of freshly grated nutmeg, using an electric grinder or pestle and mortar. Pass the mixture through a sieve and measure 5 ml (1 tsp).

SEMI-FINAL

ALISON FIANDER • ROGER HEMMING • FIONA PHELPS

PANEL OF JUDGES
Michel Bourdin • Egon Ronay • Loyd Grossman

FIONA PHELPS' MENU

STARTER

Roquefort and Spring Onion Tartlets
on a bed of Lamb's Lettuce with a Redcurrant and Walnut Dressing

"One of the best dishes I have had" **Egon Ronay**

MAIN COURSE

Baked Turbot with Mussels in a Dill and Saffron Sauce
on a bed of Steamed Leeks

Fried Julienne Potatoes

DESSERT

Apricot Mousse Brulée

Roquefort and Spring Onion Tartlets

Tartlets:
450 g (1 lb) puff pastry (preferably home-made)
225 g (8 oz) Roquefort cheese
4 spring onions, trimmed and chopped
30 ml (2 tbsp) chopped walnuts
1 egg
120 ml (4 fl oz) double cream
salt and freshly ground black pepper
freshly grated nutmeg

Redcurrant and Walnut Dressing:
45 ml (3 tbsp) olive oil
15 ml (1 tbsp) walnut oil
15 ml (1 tbsp) balsamic vinegar
7.5 ml (1½ tsp) lemon juice
2.5 ml (½ tsp) French wholegrain mustard
30 ml (2 tbsp) redcurrant jelly
45 ml (3 tbsp) chopped walnuts

To Serve:
lamb's lettuce

Roll out the pastry on a lightly floured surface and use to line 4 individual 7.5 cm (3 inch) flan tins. Prick the bases with a fork, line with greaseproof paper and baking beans and bake blind in a preheated oven at 220°C (425°F) mark 7 for 8-10 minutes until firm. Remove the paper and beans and allow to cool.

Chop the Roquefort and mix with the spring onions and walnuts. In a bowl, whisk the egg and cream together. Season with pepper, nutmeg and a little salt. Stir in the cheese mixture and spoon into the flan cases. Bake in the oven for 15 minutes until risen and golden.

Meanwhile put all of the dressing ingredients into a screw-topped jar and shake vigorously to emulsify. Toss the lamb's lettuce in the dressing, then arrange a bed on each serving plate. Place the warm tartlets on top to serve.

BAKED TURBOT WITH MUSSELS IN A DILL AND SAFFRON SAUCE

4 turbot fillets, each about 150 g (5 oz)
24 mussels, cleaned
4 lemon slices
4 dill sprigs
juice of ½ lemon
90 ml (3 fl oz) white wine
15 ml (1 tbsp) olive oil
2 shallots, chopped
15 ml (1 tbsp) chopped dill
300 ml (½ pint) fish stock
1 saffron stand
dash of dry sherry
175 ml (6 fl oz) double cream
125 g (4 oz) unsalted butter
3 leeks, trimmed and shredded
chopped herbs (dill, coriander and chervil),
* to garnish*

Skin the turbot fillets if necessary. Discard any mussels with open or damaged shells.

Place each turbot fillet in the middle of a sheet of buttered foil and top with a slice of lemon, a dill sprig, a squeeze of lemon juice and 15 ml (1 tbsp) white wine. Wrap the foil around the turbot to enclose and seal the edges well. Place in a shallow ovenproof dish, containing a little warm water and bake in a preheated oven at 180°C (350°F) mark 4 for 15 minutes, until cooked.

Meanwhile, heat the olive oil in a large pan and fry the shallots until softened. Add the remaining lemon juice, wine and chopped dill. Pour in the fish stock and add the mussels. Cover the pan tightly and cook over a high heat for about 3 minutes, shaking the pan occasionally, until the mussels open; discard any that remain closed.

Remove the mussels from the pan with a slotted spoon; place in a covered dish and keep warm. Boil the cooking liquor to reduce by about two thirds, then add the saffron, sherry and cream. Stir well, then whisk in the butter, a little at a time.

Meanwhile, steam the shredded leeks for about 3 minutes until they are cooked but still retain a bite. Drain thoroughly.

To serve, arrange a bed of leeks on each warmed serving plate. Place a turbot fillet on top. Arrange the mussels around the turbot and pour the sauce around them. Sprinkle with chopped herbs and serve immediately, accompanied by fried potato julienne.

APRICOT MOUSSE BRULÉE

Mousse:
400 ml (13½ fl oz) double cream
½ vanilla pod, split
4 egg yolks
50 g (2 oz) caster sugar
15 ml (1 tbsp) amaretto di Saronno liqueur

Coulis:
2 ripe apricots
30 g (1¼ oz) caster sugar
15 ml (1 tbsp) water
few drops of lemon juice

Praline:
150 ml (5 fl oz) caster sugar
25 ml (1 fl oz) water
30 g (1¼ oz) flaked almonds

For the mousse, put 300 ml (½ pint) of the cream in a saucepan with the split vanilla pod. Slowly bring to the boil and simmer gently for 5 minutes. Meanwhile, in a bowl whisk the egg yolks and sugar together until pale and creamy. Gradually pour on the hot cream, whisking constantly. Return to the pan and cook over a very low heat, stirring constantly, until thickened enough to lightly coat the back of the spoon. Strain into a bowl and allow to cool, then refrigerate for 2 hours.

To prepare the coulis, chop the apricots and discard the stones. Dissolve the sugar in the water over a low heat. Add the apricots and lemon juice, cover and cook for 6-8 minutes. Cool, then purée in a blender or food processor. Pass through a sieve, then place in the clean pan. Reduce until the purée thickens, whisking all the time. Let cool, then spread over the base of 4 ramekins.

To finish the mousses, whip the remaining 100 ml (3½ fl oz) cream with the liqueur until thick. Fold into the chilled mousse base, then divide between the ramekins. Return to the refrigerator.

To make the praline, dissolve the sugar in the water in a heavy-based pan over a low heat, then bring to the boil. Add the almonds and cook to a light caramel. Pour the mixture onto an oiled baking tray and leave to cool and harden.

Put the ramekins in the freezer for a few minutes. Break the praline into pieces and grind to a powder in a food processor or blender. Spread the praline evenly over the mousses and place under a preheated high grill for 30 seconds. Refrigerate for 15-30 minutes before serving.

The Final

Gerry Goldwyre • Elaine Bates • Alison Fiander

Panel of Judges

Prue Leith • Lord St John • Loyd Grossman

WINNER

Gerry Goldwyre's Menu

Starter

*Fettucine with Strips of Chicken Breast, Morels
and a Herb Sauce*

"Wonderful sauce... very earth" **Loyd**

Main Course

*Medallions of Skye Monkfish with a Trompet and Tarragon Sauce,
on a bed of Spinach, with a Potato and Courgette Topping
and Slow-roast Cherry Tomatoes*

"Absolutely sensational" **Loyd**

Dessert

*Chocolate and Wild Cherry Ice Cream,
with a Cherry and Kirsch Compote*

Tuiles

FETTUCINE WITH STRIPS OF CHICKEN BREAST, MORELS AND A HERB SAUCE

125-175 g (4-6 oz) corn-fed chicken breast
  fillet
30 ml (2 tbsp) garlic oil
finely pared rind of 1 lemon
1 tomato, skinned, seeded and diced
10 morel mushrooms
25 g (1 oz) unsalted butter

Pasta:
130 g (4½ oz) plain flour
pinch of salt
1 egg (size 2), plus 1 yolk

Sauce:
300 ml (½ pint) velouté stock (see note)
100 ml (3½ fl oz) double cream
25 g (1 oz) chopped coriander leaves
maldon salt
freshly ground white pepper

To Serve:
fine shaving of Parmesan cheese
chopped coriander leaves

Cut the chicken into thin strips and place in a bowl with the garlic oil and lemon rind. Set aside in a cool place.

To make the pasta, put the flour and salt in a food processor and, with the motor running, add the egg and egg yolk through the feeder tube. When the dough begins to come together, form into a ball, wrap in cling film and leave to rest in the refrigerator for 30 minutes.

Roll out the pasta dough a quarter at a time, keeping the other portions wrapped. Flatten the dough and pass it through the pasta machine repeatedly, gradually narrowing the gap between the rollers each time to roll thinly until you reach the last but one setting. Feed the pasta through the wider set of cutters to make fettucine.

Fry the mushrooms in the butter for 2-3 minutes; set aside. For the sauce, bring the stock to the boil in a saucepan, add the cream and return to the boil. Stir in the chopped coriander and adjust the seasoning just before serving.

Cook the tagliatelle in a large pan of boiling salted water for 2-3 minutes until al dente. Drain thoroughly and add to the sauce with the mushrooms and tomato; heat through briefly. Meanwhile place a heavy-based frying pan over a high heat and quickly fry the chicken strips until tender. Add to the pasta.

Divide between warmed individual serving bowls and top with slivers of Parmesan cheese and coriander leaves. Serve immediately.

Note: For the velouté stock, use a well-flavoured, slightly thickened, chicken stock.

MEDALLIONS OF SKYE MONKFISH WITH A TROMPET AND TARRAGON SAUCE

700 g (1½ lb) monkfish
16 cherry tomatoes
25 g (1 oz) dried trompets (or other dried
mushrooms)
300 ml (½ pint) wine fish stock
200 ml (⅓ pint) double cream
maldon salt
freshly ground white pepper
175 g (6 oz) spinach, thoroughly cleaned
tiny knob of butter
lemon juice, to taste
40 g (1½ oz) tarragon, chopped

Potato and Courgette Topping:
175 g (6 oz) potatoes, peeled
2 courgettes
oil for deep-frying

Cut the monkfish into medallions, ½ -1 cm (¼ -½ inch) thick, and pat dry with kitchen paper; cover and set aside in a cool place.

Place the cherry tomatoes on an oiled baking tray and roast in a preheated oven at 150°C (300°F) mark 2 for 2-3 hours.

Meanwhile soak the mushrooms in warm water to cover for 20 minutes. Transfer to a small pan and cook until the mushrooms are tender and the liquid has evaporated. In another pan, heat the fish stock. Stir in the cream and adjust the seasoning. Add the mushrooms to the sauce.

To prepare the potato and courgette topping, using a vegetable peeler, finely pare thin strips from the potatoes. Repeat with the courgettes. Pat dry with kitchen paper. Heat the oil in a deep-fryer to 190°C (375°F). Add the potato strips and fry until they just stop bubbling and begin to change colour. Remove and drain on kitchen paper; keep warm. Repeat with the courgette strips; keep warm.

Remove any tough stalks from the spinach. Place a frying pan over moderate heat. Add the butter, then the spinach and cook, turning constantly, until tender. Season with salt and pepper, and add lemon juice to taste. Set aside; keep warm.

To cook the monkfish, place a heavy-based frying pan over a high heat. Add a few drops of oil, then place the fish medallions in the pan, moving them a little initially to prevent sticking (then don't move again). Cook for about 1 minute, then turn and cook for 45 seconds. (The cooking time will depend on the thickness of the fish.) Season with salt and pepper, and sprinkle with a little lemon juice; keep warm.

Bring the sauce to the boil and stir in the chopped tarragon. Place a bed of spinach on each warmed serving plate and arrange the monkfish on top. Place 2 cherry tomatoes at each end of the fish and pour the sauce around. Sprinkle the crispy courgette and potatoes on top of the fish. Serve immediately.

CHOCOLATE AND WILD CHERRY ICE CREAM, WITH A CHERRY COMPOTE

For the compote, you will need to soak the dried cherries in the kirsch at least overnight, or preferably for 24 hours.

Ice Cream:
90 g (3½ oz) quality dark chocolate
15 ml (1 tbsp) caster sugar
45 ml (3 tbsp) water
2 egg yolks
150 ml (¼ pint) milk (at room temperature)
150 ml (¼ pint) double cream (at room temperature)
15 g (½ oz) dried American wild cherries

Compote:
50 g (2 oz) dried cherries soaked in 45 ml (3 tbsp) kirsch
45 ml (3 tbsp) caster sugar
45 ml (3 tbsp) water
squeeze of lemon juice

To Serve:
chocolate curls
Tuiles (see right)

Grate 15 g (½ oz) of the chocolate and set aside in a cool place. Break the rest into pieces and place in a bowl over a pan of hot water until melted. Stir in the milk and cream.

Meanwhile, dissolve the sugar in the water in a small pan over a low heat, then bring to the boil and simmer for 1 minute. Set aside to cool.

In a bowl, whisk the egg yolks until pale and creamy. Pour on the syrup in a steady stream, whisking constantly until the mixture begins to stiffen. Add the melted chocolate mixture and mix well, then stir in the cherries and grated chocolate.

Transfer to an ice-cream maker and churn until firm. Unless serving immediately, transfer to a freezerproof container and store in the freezer.

To prepare the compote, dissolve the sugar in the water in a small pan over a low heat, then bring to the boil and simmer for 1 minute. Add the kirsch marinade from the cherries and mix well, then add a squeeze of lemon juice. Stir the cherries into the sauce.

To serve, scoop the ice cream onto chilled plates and sprinkle with chocolate curls. Arrange 3 tuiles around each serving and place spoonfuls of cherry compote between them. Serve at once.

Note: If you do not have an ice-cream maker, freeze the ice-cream in a suitable container, whisking periodically during freezing to break down the ice crystals.

TUILES

125 g (4 oz) plain flour
125 g (4 oz) icing sugar
1 egg white (size 1)
65 g (2½ oz) butter, melted

Sift the flour and icing sugar into a bowl. Whisk in the egg white, then pour on the melted butter and whisk until smooth. Leave to rest in the refrigerator for 20 minutes.

Place 3 or 4 spoonfuls of the batter on a greased baking sheet, spacing them well apart, and spread thinly into rounds with the back of the spoon. Bake in a preheated oven at 190°C (375°F) mark 5 for about 3 minutes until golden. Whilst still warm, mould each biscuit over a narrow rolling pin or wooden spoon handle to form a half cylinder shape. Carefully remove and cool on a wire rack. Repeat with the remaining batter to make 12 tuiles in total.

The Final

Gerry Goldwyre • Elaine Bates • Alison Fiander

PANEL OF JUDGES
Prue Leith • Lord St John • Loyd Grossman

ELAINE BATES' MENU

STARTER
Light Crab Bisque served with its Meat

MAIN COURSE
Fillet of Beef poached in St Emilion with a Confit of Shallots
"Absolutely beyond reproach" **Loyd**
Miniature Yorkshire Puddings
Savoy Cabbage
Shredded Carrots and Jerusalem Artichokes

DESSERT
*Pan-fried Apples, Pears and Hazelnuts
with Vanilla and Caramel Crèmes*

LIGHT CRAB BISQUE

1 cooked crab, weighing about 700 g (1½ lb)
60 ml (4 tbsp) olive oil
1 stick celery, sliced
1 small onion, chopped
1 leek, diced
1 carrot, diced
60 ml (4 tbsp) sherry
450 g (1 lb) tomatoes, chopped
½ bottle medium white wine
300 ml (½ pint) water
pinch of saffron strands
salt and freshly ground white pepper
50 g (2 oz) plain flour
50 g (2 oz) butter, softened

Scrub the crab thoroughly under cold water to rid it of any remaining grit. Discard the inedible dead man's fingers and stomach sac from the crab (if not already done). Break off the claws and extract all of the white meat. Using a teaspoon, scoop out into separate bowls the white and dark meat from the shell. Break the shell into pieces and reserve.

Heat the olive oil in a large pan, add the celery, onion, leek and carrot and sauté until softened. Add the pieces of crab shell and sauté for 2 minutes. Add the sherry and allow it to evaporate. Add the tomatoes, wine, water, brown crabmeat and saffron and bring to the boil. Reduce the heat and simmer for 45 minutes.

Strain through a fine sieve into a clean saucepan, pressing hard to extract all of the juices. Bring back to the boil and season with salt and pepper to taste. Blend the flour into the softened butter to make a beurre manie and gradually whisk into the bisque, a piece at a time, until slightly thickened.

To serve, divide the white crabmeat between warmed soup plates, then pour on the bisque.

FILLET OF BEEF POACHED IN ST EMILION WITH A CONFIT OF SHALLOTS

450 g (1 lb) pink shallots
50 g (2 oz) unsalted butter
30 ml (2 tbsp) olive oil
1 bottle of St Emilion, or other full-bodied
 red wine
450 g (1 lb) fillet of beef, in one piece
1 carrot, sliced
2 pieces streaky bacon, derinded and
 chopped
1 thyme sprig
600 ml (1 pint) beef stock
salt and freshly ground black pepper

Finely slice the shallots, reserving 15 ml (1 tbsp) for later. In a small saucepan, melt 25 g (1 oz) of the butter with 15 ml (1 tbsp) of the olive oil. Add the shallots and cook until beginning to soften and turn golden. Increase the heat and add 150 ml (¼ pint) of the wine. Bring to the boil, then simmer over a very low heat for about 45 minutes until the shallots have absorbed all of the wine and are very soft.

Meanwhile, heat the remaining oil in a large heavy-based pan. Add the beef and seal on all sides over a high heat, then remove. Add the reserved spoonful of shallots to the pan with the carrot, bacon and thyme; fry until browned. Add half the remaining wine, bring to the boil and reduce by half. Strain into a small saucepan and reserve for the sauce.

Meanwhile, pour the stock and remaining wine into a large saucepan and bring to the boil. Add the beef, reduce the heat to a gentle simmer and cook for about 10-15 minutes, depending on the thickness of the meat; it should still be pink in the middle. Lift out the meat, cover with foil and leave to rest for 15 minutes.

Reheat the wine reduction reserved

for the sauce and add a similar amount of cooking liquid from the beef. Reduce again until a good consistency is obtained and taste for seasoning. Whisk in a knob of butter.

To serve, slice the beef into 12 thin rounds. Place a mound of shallots in the centre of each serving plate and arrange three slices of beef around each one. Place three Yorkshire puddings on each plate, then pour the sauce around. Serve with Savoy cabbage and the shredded carrors and artichokes.

Note: A good full-bodied wine is essential for this dish.

MINIATURE YORKSHIRE PUDDINGS

110 g (4 oz) strong plain flour
salt and freshly ground black pepper
1 egg, beaten
150 ml (¼ pint) milk
90 ml (3 fl oz) water
beef dripping, for cooking

Put the flour into a bowl and season with salt and pepper. Make a well in the centre and add the egg. Gradually mix the egg into the flour, then add the milk and water and mix to a smooth batter. Allow to stand for at least 30 minutes.

Put a small amount of dripping into each of 12 miniature patty tins – about 2.5 cm (1 inch) in diameter. Place in a preheated oven at 220°C (425°F) mark 7 for 5 minutes until sizzling. Pour the batter mixture into the patty tins and cook in the oven for 10 minutes or until well risen and golden brown.

SHREDDED CARROTS AND JERUSALEM ARTICHOKES

225 g (8 oz) carrots
225 g (8 oz) Jerusalem artichokes
knob of butter
5 ml (1 tsp) mustard seeds
5 ml (1 tsp) Dijon mustard
15 ml (1 tbsp) single cream
freshly ground black pepper

Peel the carrots and Jerusalem artichokes, then shred using a food processor. Place in a saucepan with the butter, 15 ml (1 tbsp) water and the mustard seeds. Heat through gently for a couple of minutes. Mix the mustard and cream together and stir into the mixture. Season with pepper and serve at once.

PAN-FRIED APPLES, PEARS AND HAZELNUTS WITH VANILLA AND CARAMEL CRÈMES

2 apples
2 ripe pears
juice of ½ lemon
12 Cape gooseberries
125 g (4 oz) unsalted butter
125 g (4 oz) caster sugar
½ vanilla pod, split
50 g (2 oz) shelled hazelnuts

Vanilla and Caramel Crèmes:
175 ml (6 fl oz) milk
175 ml (6 fl oz) single cream
½ vanilla pod
175 g (6 oz) sugar
90 ml (3 fl oz) water
2 eggs, plus 2 egg yolks

To Decorate:
4 Cape gooseberries

First prepare the crèmes. Heat the milk and cream together in a saucepan with the vanilla pod to just below the boil. Remove from the heat and leave to infuse for 10 minutes. Meanwhile, dissolve 125 g (4 oz) sugar with the water in a small heavy-based saucepan over a low heat. Increase the heat and cook to a light golden caramel. Remove from the heat and carefully stir in 15 ml (1 tbsp) cold water. Allow to cool slightly.

Meanwhile, whisk 1 egg and 1 egg yolk with the remaining 50 g (2 oz) sugar. Pour on two thirds of the infused milk mixture and strain into 2 ramekin dishes.

Whisk the remaining egg and egg yolk together. Add the rest of the milk to the caramel and stir until combined, then pour onto the whisked eggs. Strain this into another 2 ramekins.

Stand the ramekins in a bain-marie or roasting tin containing enough hot water to come halfway up the sides of the dishes. Bake in a preheated oven at 180°C (350°F) mark 4 for about 15 minutes until just lightly set. Allow to cool.

Peel and core the apples and pears, then cut into quarters and sprinkle with the lemon juice to prevent discolouration. Remove the husks from the Cape gooseberries, but leave whole.

In a non-stick pan large enough to take the fruits in a single layer, melt the butter and sugar together. Add the vanilla pod, apples and pears. Cook gently until tender and very lightly golden, adding the Cape gooseberries and hazelnuts a few minutes before the end of the cooking. Baste the fruits with the pan juices during cooking.

Divide the cooked fruit and nuts between individual serving dishes, including some of the cooking juices. Place two small spoonfuls of each crème on one side of each dish. Decorate each dessert with a Cape gooseberry in its papery husk. Serve at once.

The Final

Gerry Goldwyre • Elaine Bates • Alison Fiander

Panel of Judges

Prue Leith • Lord St John • Loyd Grossman

Alison Fiander's Menu

Starter

Butternut Squash Ravioli with Sage Butter

Main Course

Tuscan-style Venison
Creamed Potatoes with Chives
Green Beans

Dessert

Raspberry and Chianti Sorbet
"Brilliant pudding" **Loyd**

BUTTERNUT SQUASH RAVIOLI WITH SAGE BUTTER

The quantities for the filling make more than you need for the ravioli. Freeze the leftover filling for another occasion.

Pasta:
300 g (10 oz) type '00' pasta flour
pinch of salt
3 eggs (size 3)
15 ml (1 tbsp) oil
beaten egg, to seal (optional)

Filling:
1 butternut squash
olive oil, for basting
salt and freshly ground black pepper
3 amaretti biscuits
75 g (3 oz) Parmesan cheese, freshly grated
125 g (4 oz) canned mustard fruits, chopped (see note)
freshly grated nutmeg

Sage Butter Sauce:
100 g (3½ oz) butter
large handful (½ cup) sage leaves

To Serve:
freshly grated Parmesan cheese

First prepare the filling. Cut the unpeeled butternut squash into large pieces, discarding the seeds. Toss in olive oil and season with salt and pepper. Roast in a preheated oven at 180°C (350°F) mark 4 for 1½ hours or until cooked. When cool enough to handle, peel the squash.

Grind the amaretti biscuits in a food processor, then add the squash, Parmesan, mustard fruits, nutmeg and seasoning. Blend thoroughly.

To make the pasta, sift the flour and salt onto a clean surface, make a well in the centre and add the eggs and oil. Gradually work the flour into the eggs, using your hands to mix to a firm, pliable dough. Knead thoroughly on a lightly floured surface until smooth. Wrap tightly in cling film and leave to rest for 1 hour.

Roll out the dough (about a quarter at a time), using a pasta machine. Pass the dough through the machine repeatedly, narrowing the setting each time until the pasta is a thin sheet. Lay one sheet of pasta on the work surface and spoon on heaped teaspoonfuls of stuffing at 5 cm (2 inch) intervals. Brush the edges of the pasta and between the filling with a little beaten egg if necessary (see note). Cover with another sheet of pasta and press along the edges and between the stuffing to seal. Using a 5 cm (2 inch) fluted round cutter, cut out the ravioli; make sure the edges are well sealed. Repeat with the rest of the dough and filling.

Cook the ravioli in a large pan of boiling water for about 5 minutes until *al dente*. Meanwhile make the sauce. Melt the butter in a pan, add the sage leaves and cook until they are crisp. Drain the cooked ravioli, arrange on warmed serving plates and pour on the sage butter sauce. Sprinkle with Parmesan to serve.

Note: Mustard fruits are available in cans from Italian delicatessens. They comprise a mixture of peaches, pears, cherries, etc, preserved in a mustardy syrup. Use a mixture of the different fruits for the ravioli filling.

You may find that the pasta edges adhere perfectly well without beaten egg. If you do not have a pasta machine, roll out the pasta as thinly as possible on a clean surface.

TUSCAN-STYLE VENISON

15 g (½ oz) dried porcini mushrooms
700-900 g (1½-2 lb) venison
salt and freshly ground black pepper
flour, for coating
olive oil and butter, for cooking
125 g (4 oz) pancetta, derinded and chopped
1-2 cloves garlic, chopped
2 onions, finely chopped
2 carrots, finely chopped
2 sticks celery, finely chopped
500 ml (16 fl oz) dry red wine
500 ml (16 fl oz) passata
a little stock (optional)

Dolce Forte:
125 ml (4 fl oz) red wine vinegar
40 g (1½ oz) raisins
25 g (1 oz) pine nuts
40 g (1½ oz) plain chocolate chips
15 ml (1 tbsp) sugar

Soak the dried porcini in 150 ml (¼ pint) hot water for 20 minutes; drain.

Cut the venison into chunks and toss in seasoned flour to coat. Heat some olive oil and butter together in a heavy-based pan or braising pot, then brown the venison in batches on all sides, adding more oil and butter as necessary. Remove and set aside.

Add the pancetta and the garlic to the pan and sauté briefly, then add the oinions and sauté for a few minutes. Add the porcini, carrots and celery and cook, stirring, for a few minutes. Add the red wine and cook for about 5 minutes. Stir in the passata and cook, uncovered, for about 15 minutes.

Return the venison to the pan and cook for 15 minutes. Add the *dolce forte* ingredients and cook for a further 5 minutes. Leave the lid off the pot throughout the cooking time. If the sauce is too thick, thin with a little stock.

Serve accompanied by creamed potatoes flavoured with snipped chives, and green beans.

Raspberry and Chianti Sorbet

225 g (8 oz) caster sugar
1 bottle of Chianti, or similar red wine
12 mint leaves
300 g (10 oz) frozen raspberries

Dissolve the sugar in the wine in a saucepan over a low heat. Increase the heat, add the mint leaves and boil for about 2 minutes. Remove from the heat, add the raspberries and leave to stand for 1 hour.

Discard the mint leaves, then purée the raspberries and wine syrup in a blender or food processor. Strain through a nylon sieve to remove pips.

Transfer the mixture to an ice-cream machine and churn until frozen, then transfer to the freezer (unless serving imediately). If you do not have an ice-cream maker, freeze the sorbet in a freezerproof container, whisking periodically during freezing to break down the ice crystals and ensure a smooth result.

To serve, scoop the sorbet into chilled serving dishes. Serve at once.

INDEX

OF RECIPE TITLES AND CONTESTANTS